Clinical Social Workers
as Psychotherapists

GARDNER PRESS SERIES IN CLINICAL SOCIAL WORK
MARY GOTTESFELD, M.S.W., Editor

SEPARATION-INDIVIDUATION: Theory and Application
By Joyce Edward, Nathene Ruskin, Patsy Turrini

EXISTENTIAL PSYCHOTHERAPY: The Process of Caring
By David G. Edwards

CLINICAL SOCIAL WORKERS AS PSYCHOTHERAPISTS
Edited by Florence Lieberman

Clinical Social Workers as Psychotherapists

Edited By
FLORENCE LIEBERMAN, D.S.W.
Hunter College

GARDNER PRESS, INC.
New York

Gardner Press, Inc.
19 Union Square West
New York 10003

Library of Congress Cataloging in Publication Data
Main entry under title:
Clinical social workers as psychotherapists.
    Bibliography: p.
    Includes index.
        1. Psychiatric social work—Addresses, essays, lectures.
    2. Psychotherapy—Social aspects—Addresses, essays, lectures.
    I. Lieberman, Florence.
    HV689.C55   362.2'04256   82-3019
    ISBN 0-89876-037-2   AACR2

Printed in the United States of America

Design by Publishers Creative Services Inc.

In Memory of Helen Pinkus, D.S.W.
Social Worker
Teacher and Friend to Many

HELEN PINKUS and I met through activities in the National Federation of Societies for Clinical Social Work, where both of us shared an interest in quality clinical social work. Helen chaired the Education Committee of the Federation. As we worked on issues relating to the nature of clinical social work practice, we found much congruence in our viewpoints. We respected the abilities of social workers and prized a theoretical rationale for creative, individualized clinical interventions. We believed that good clinical social work is psychotherapy. Above all, we were proud of our social foundations and our social work profession.

The decision to recognize the work of practitioners by publishing their papers in a book evolved from these feelings. We decided we would secure new examples of clinical work that would be representative of social work psychotherapy and that would demonstrate that psychotherapy was taking place in the many diverse settings in which clinical social workers practice, and with the widespread population groups with which clinical social workers are involved. Obviously, we could not reflect everything that was done. We planned to provide a beginning sample.

Then Helen became ill and died.

We had become friends during this professional association. We had dined together, visited together, and talked of many things. One of Helen's memorable characteristics was that she always told you what she thought. She was honest and forthright. Sometimes, at meetings, when I would stray from the subject, she would call me to attention. During the long period of putting this book together, I have often thought: "What would Helen think of this?"

Florence Lieberman

Acknowledgments

This book was encouraged by the leadership and membership of the National Federation of Societies for Clinical Social Work. Two of the purposes of the Federation as stated in its Bylaws are:

To advance and promote the profession and practice of clinical social work by assisting the State and/or Regional Societies for Clinical Social Work in establishing and maintaining high standards of professional education, practice, ethics, and achievement;

To increase and disseminate professional knowledge through research, reports, discussion, and publications.

As chairperson of the Federation's Education Committee I have had the opportunity to learn of thoughtful, innovative clinical social work practice throughout the United States and in many diverse settings. This inspired the wish to share this knowledge with the larger community. Obviously this small volume does not describe adequately or fully the creative work performed by members of the Federation; this has yet to be done. However, gratitude is tendered to all of those who inspired this book by sharing their practice and to the various state societies that also shared their efforts in the area of continued education.

Mary Gottesfeld, editor of this series of books in social work, colleague, and friend, offered special assistance through her criticisms and suggestions.

I would also like to thank David Feldstein, colleague at Hunter College School of Social Work, for his invaluable review of the first chapter, "Psychotherapy and Social Work."

Florence Lieberman

Contents

In Memory of Helen Pinkus, D.S.W.   *v*
   Florence Lieberman
Acknowledgments   *vii*
Foreword by Florence Hollis   *xi*
Contributors   *xvii*

Part One: Foundations

1. Psychotherapy and Social Work   *3*
   Florence Lieberman
2. Social Work Contributions to Psychotherapy   *21*
   Marcella Baird
3. Beyond the Master's Degree: Education for Social   *37*
   Work Psychotherapy
   Education Committee, N.F.S.C.S.W.
4. Psychoanalysis and Social Work: A Re-examination   *51*
   of the Issues
   Selma Fraiberg

Part Two: Adults

5. The Invited Guest in a Mother's Therapy: Fostering   *73*
   Symbolic Recapitulation of Developmental Conflict
   Mary L. Gottesfeld
6. Reparation After the Countertransference   *79*
   Terry de Groot
7. Marital Couples in Stress: Therapeutic Strategy   *91*
   Elsie Herman
8. Criminal Offenders: The Dilemma of Involuntary   *109*
   Treatment
   Cheryl Gropper and Janice Zolman Bogner

Part Three: Adolescents and Children

9. The Mixed-Age Group as an Adolescent's Transitional   *125*
   Family
   Florence Lieberman

10. Treatment of an Adolescent from a Multiproblem Family   *137*
    Harriet Mauer

11. Narcissism and Hyperaggressiveness: A Study of   *151*
    Hyperaggressive Borderline Children
    Crayton E. Rowe, Jr.

12. Childhood Phobia and Family Therapy: *165*
    A Case Illustration
    Mary E. Woods

Subject Index   *179*

Author Index   *187*

FOREWORD

Clinical Social Workers as Psychotherapists, developed from the plans of Helen Pinkus and Florence Lieberman, does indeed fulfill their purpose of using the work of practitioners to demonstrate the depth and breadth of clinical social work and its place among the psychotherapies.

Clinical social work is emerging from a period of internal experimentation with a variety of approaches of seemingly conflicting types of therapy and a period of denigration and neglect within the general social work field.

The evaluative research of the fifties, sixties, and even seventies, with its often discouraging findings, is itself now being evaluated. It is rightfully seen by many modern clinical researchers as a perhaps necessary and useful stage of research development but (Fischer to the contrary) far too gross and fallacious a measuring instrument to be relied upon to give an accurate and useful picture of either the process or the results of clinical social work. Fortunately, more advanced methods are now being developed to carry out this most necessary function better.

Direct-service practitioners have begun to press for recognition of the fact, long recognized by skilled practitioners, that work with people having complex psychosocial problems requires intensive training specifically for this task. To a great extent this is also true of clinical research. Until the 1950s training for the practice of casework was the predominant form of study in almost all schools of social work. This included extensive field work practice in agencies dealing with clients having psychosocial dilemmas. As early as 1940 it was recognized that this amount of concentration did not provide the degree of skill required for helping individuals with many types of personal problems, especially marital and parent–child difficulties, and problems of personal adjustment.

The generic education theme that came forward in these early years referred to the commonalities inherent in the practice of casework in various settings, for example, family, medical, psychiatric, and child welfare. In the fifties, with the expansion of American Association of Social Workers to National Association of Social Workers and the gradual abandonment of the smaller professional societies such as AAPSW and AAMSW, the pendulum swung under new leadership to emphasis on social change. For a number of crucial years, when other professions were growing in their contributions to the field of psychotherapy, NASW gave little support to the concerns of direct service practitioners.

More recently, with the emergence of the National Federation of Societies of Clinical Social Workers, NASW has awakened to the needs of its clinically oriented members and has itself established a national register of clinical social workers, as well as offering an increasing number of programs in which such workers' interests and concerns are heeded.

Meanwhile, the Federation has begun to assert itself in the educational field and in the general field of psychotherapy. The article, "Education for the Practice of Clinical Social Work at the Master's Level: A Position Paper," written primarily by Helen Pinkus[1] and published in 1977, was the first to express the opinions of the Federation's leaders on the essentials of educational preparation for clinical social work.

The present volume carries forward the task of reestablishing clinical social work in its rightful place as a promising form of psychosocial treatment correctly designated as psychotherapy. Part One, consisting of the first four chapters grouped together as "Foundations," deals with general issues concerning social work psychotherapy and training for its practice.

The point is well made and well substantiated that social work is one of the earliest professions offering psychological as well as social treatment. Numerically, its practitioners were for many decades the largest group—except perhaps for psychiatry—professionally trained for such practice. Even today, despite the growth of other clinical groups, it does the greater part of the work in psychiatric and community mental health clinics.

Chapter 2 is convincing in its argument that social work's emphasis on the intermeshing of psychological and social components in all human problems has made a major contribution to the general field of psychotherapy. This duality was recognized very early by caseworkers—certainly by the 1920s—and has been incorporated

---

1. Pinkus, H., Haring, J., Lieberman, F., Mishne, J., and Pollack, J. Education for the Practice of Clinical Social Work at the Master's Level: A Position Paper. *Clinical Social Work Journal*, 1977, 5, 251–268.

in varying degrees by most modern practitioners in all fields of psychotherapy.

Chapter 3 deals with the question of advanced education for social work psychotherapy and definitely spells out the need for post-master's clinical programs under both academic and practice sectors of the profession. The chapter takes the position that academic auspices are preferable, provided that schools of social work employ for this purpose faculty members with concurrent clinical experience.

Chapter 4, written from the vantage point of a social worker also trained in psychoanalysis, demonstrates the possibility of combining these two approaches in a setting where both proceed from similar basic principles to offer a service of very high quality.

Parts Two and Three present illustrations and discussions of clinical work with adults, adolescents, and children. These chapters are not meant to give an exhaustive picture of these fields, but rather to describe a variety of psychological and social problems and various procedures that different practitioners in different settings have found useful in alleviating the distress caused by such problems, thus enabling people to cope with them more effectively.

In Chapter 5 we see a flexible therapist acceding to the wish of a mother, diagnosed as suffering from a narcissistic personality disorder, to have her infant with her during treatment. With the help of the child's presence, it was possible for a symbiotic mother–child relationship to develop between client and therapist, which enabled the client to rework her conflict with individuation. Through this the client gained a new ability both to relate to her child and later to separate from her, thus freeing the child for more normal development. This theme of separation–individuation appears again in Chapter 6, with emphasis on the positive use of the transference.

Chapter 7 gives a broad view of marital problems, using both systems theory concepts with stress on the factor of equilibrium, and dynamic psychology, stressing the necessity for understanding the feelings and psychology of both partners. The use of individual, family, and group interviews is discussed. The importance of study assessment as the basis for definitive therapeutic plans and constant reassessment is emphasized.

The difficult question of involuntary treatment is dealt with in Chapter 8. Use of the client's resistance itself through empathic recognition of it is stressed as a good device for beginning to work through such resistance. The problem of countertransference is recognized as a major factor to be watched carefully.

The succeeding chapters in Part three explore work with adolescents and children and form a highly useful section of the book. Chapter 9 describes an unusual form of group treatment in which an adolescent is included in groups consisting primarily of adults. It is found that a heterogeneous group can sometimes serve as an alternative transitional family for disturbed adolescents who have internalized their family's pathology. Again, case material with an older adolescent demonstrates the process and its usefulness.

In Chapter 10 we see work with an attractive girl of high intelligence from a multiple-problem family with "multigenerational role-reversal patterna." Much practical work is involved with the family, as well as interviews over several years with the at first highly anxious, ambivalent, and resistive adolescent.

The next two chapters deal with the younger child. Appropriately, Chapter 11 leads off with a discussion of narcissism and hyperaggressiveness. Two dramatic case illustrations demonstrate flexible and imaginative work with hyperaggressive children defending themselves from primitive forms of identification by archaic ideation. The contribution of discouraging environments is given appropriate weight in the theoretical discussion.

Chapter 12, on the other hand, describes a child with a recently appearing neurotic symptom. After a number of sessions, and with difficulty, a "family secret" is finally brought to light that is both directly and indirectly responsible for the child's fears. A good case is made for the value of dealing with these factors rather than limiting treatment to reduction of the phobia itself.

This is the book that Helen Pinkus dreamed of but could not bring to completion.

It is a great pity that Helen Pinkus' life was cut short at such an early age. She was one of the best spokespersons for clinical research. Genuine and forthright, she thought and wrote clearly. Without being dogmatic, she was thoroughly grounded in the main casework stream. Helen was loved and respected both by students and by her colleagues at Smith, where she taught for so long in the tradition of Bertha Reynolds, Annette Garrett, and Florence Day.

Helen was not a mild person. There was always snap and zest and humor in her way of life. I knew her both as colleague and as doctoral student. She never hesitated to express contrary or divergent opinions. Yet one always felt such sincerity and warmth that one could not but be attracted to her as well as take her opinions seriously. Those of us who were fortunate enough to know her well feel her absence keenly.

A testimonial to the clinical social work practitioner, this book expresses Helen Pinkus' deep commitment to practice. As the different chapters integrate intricate theoretical formulations into simple practice activities, there is affirmation of her belief that theory should enhance practice, and practice should inform theory.

In this book clinical social workers salute Helen Pinkus and the values, standards, and practice to which she dedicated herself.

Florence Hollis, D.S.W.

Contributors

MARCELLA BAIRD, M.A. is in private practice in Ohio. She has worked in family service, foster care and mental retardation, and has been chief social worker in general and psychiatric hospitals, as well as Director of Admissions for Adult Service at the Menninger Foundation.

JANICE ZOLMAN BOGNER, M.S.W., is an assistant professor of clinical social work in the Department of Psychiatry, University of Cincinnati College of Medicine, and Director of Psychiatric Social Services at the University of Cincinnati Hospital, General Division.

TERRY DE GROOT, M.S.W., who is in private practice in New York, has worked as director of an outpatient clinic of a psychiatric hospital.

SELMA FRAIBERG, M.S.W., had a long history of outstanding contributions to the fields of social work, psychotherapy, and psychoanalysis. At the time of her death she was professor in the Department of Psychiatry and Pediatrics, University of California. Prior to that she was professor of child psychoanalysis and Director, Child Development Project, University Hospital, Ann Arbor, Michigan.

MARY L. GOTTESFELD, M.S.S., is coordinator of the certificate program for individual therapy of the Post-Masters Program in Advanced Clinical Social Work at the Hunter College School of Social Work. She is past editor and founder of the *Clinical Social Work Journal.* She is in private practice in New York.

ELIZABETH GRAY, M.S.S., is a consultant and part-time assistant professor of clinical social work at the University of Kansas School of Social Work. She has had over 24 years of experience as a psychotherapist and as Director of Wyandot Mental Health Center, Kansas City, Kansas.

ROBERTA S. GREENE, Ph. D., is a school social worker in Washington, D.C., and also is in private practice in Montgomery County, Maryland. She has taught in the continuing education program at Howard University School of Social Work and in adult education at the University of Maryland.

CHERYL LYNN GROPPER, M.S.W., is adjunct assistant professor of clinical social work in the Department of Psychiatry at the University of Cincinnati College of Medicine, Child Division, Central Psychiatric Clinic.

ELSIE HERMAN, M.A., is an associate professor, School of Social Work, San Diego State University, and is a consultant and in private practice. Her background is in public welfare, medical, and psychiatric social work and family and children's services.

JILL ISSELHARD, M.S.W., is in her fourth year of study at the Child and Adolescent Psychoanalytic Therapy Program of the Chicago Institute for Psychoanalysis and is in private practice. Her background is in individual treatment in family service and child welfare and as consultant in child development and parent enrichment.

BERT L. KAPLAN, Ed. D., is director of the Behavioral Sciences Division of the Adelphi University School of Social Work, is in private practice, and is a social work consultant to residential treatment center for adolescent girls.

THOMAS KENEMORE, A.M., is an assistant professor, Loyola University of Chicago, School of Social Work, a therapist at the Early Childhood Development Center, Illinois Children's Home and Aid Society, and in private practice.

FLORENCE LIEBERMAN, D.S.W., is a professor at the Hunter College School of Social Work of the City University of New York, is on the planning committee and in charge of faculty recruitment and evaluation of the Post-Masters Program in Advanced Clinical Social Work of Hunter College School of Social Work, and is in private practice. Her background is in welfare and child guidance.

HARRIET MAUER, M.S.W., is Director of Social Services, Sisters of Good Shepherd Residences, New York City, and is in private practice.

TRUDY PERSKY, M.S.W., is Mental health Consultant, DADMHA Division of Public Services, Region III and is in private practice in Philadelphia. Her background is in outpatient psychiatry, as chief social worker of Eleanor Roosevelt Health and Guidance Center, as training director of a community mental health center, and as grant coordinator for the Chicago region of the State of Illinois Department of Mental Health.

CRAYTON E. ROWE, JR., M.S.W., is past president of the National Federation of Societies for Clinical Social Work. He is an adjunct associate professor of social work at the New York University School of Social Work, supervisor and member of in-service training at University Settlement Consultation Center, New York, and in private practice.

MATILDA S. RUBIN, M.S.W., is in private practice in Michigan. Her 35 years of experience include administration, supervision, direct case work, and group therapy with the aged, the handicapped, released mental patients, and individuals and families.

MARY E. WOODS, M.S.W., is in private practice in New York. Her background includes direct service in child protection, family service, supervision, and program development.

Part One
FOUNDATIONS

FLORENCE LIEBERMAN

1

Psychotherapy and Social Work

Mrs. Jones entered psychotherapy after her mastectomy. When she applied to Group Health Incorporated for payment of her psychotherapy expenses, she received the following reply: "Your contract does not cover frames unless supplied in conjunction with lenses." Mr. Brown's request for psychotherapy payments was denied by Metropolitan Life Insurance Company, Group Health Claims, for the following reason: "Take-home drugs are not covered."

WHAT IS PSYCHOTHERAPY?

There is a plethora of definitions of psychotherapy. Despite this it is a nebulous term; the field of psychotherapy, still in flux, sometimes appears chaotic (Gunderson and Mosher, 1975; Bruch, 1974; Bergin and Strupp, 1972). It has been suggested that the concept has been broadened to such an extent that nearly every professional interaction between two people, or groups of people, is referred to as therapy (Bruch, 1974). In preparation for a meeting of the American Orthopsychiatric Association in 1948, 40 definitions of psychotherapy were collected (Garrett, 1949); and Wolberg (1977) lists at least as many in his discussion of psychotherapy. Ford and Urban (1963), limiting their comparison of major systems of psychotherapy to individual verbal psychotherapy, selected ten "to represent the great variety of theories extant in the field of psychotherapy"

3

(p.vii). Another commentator totaled a minimum of 100 types of psychotherapy (Marshall, 1980 a, b). It is almost as if each type created its own definition.

Some of the proliferation of psychotherapies may be attributed to cultural trends that have influenced the goals, types, and nature of this treatment. Marmor (1978) delineates three cultural movements within the past 25 years. Describing the counterculture movement, which evolved from disillusionment with a technology that threatens human existence with nuclear annihilation and exhaustion of natural resources, as anti-intellectual, antiscientific, and antitechnological, he suggests it has looked for answers outside of the scientific, intellectual paradigm through a variety of self-help or emotional therapies. Moreover, a conflicting emphasis on technology has led to techniques of biofeedback, audiovisual assistants, computers, and psychopharmacological aids. Finally, at the same time, cultural and socioeconomic influences have developed a growing acceptance of the relevance of psychotherapy for the treatment of emotional distress, a growing emphasis on the right to treatment, and an increasing demand for access to treatment by people from all economic levels.

The most dominant psychotherapies are grouped as psychodynamic, humanistic, or phenomenologic and behavioral. The differences among them have been attributed to variations in beliefs and values about people (Strean, 1978), theoretical viewpoints (Bergin and Strupp, 1972; Ford and Urban, 1963), and definitions of pathology. These are often expressed via varying prescriptions for the role, training, education, and techniques of the psychotherapist. Differences may occur even within therapies sharing the same theoretical orientation or technique or method. As a result, it becomes apparent that the processes of psychotherapy are neither coequal nor comfortable under a unitary term (Truax and Carkhuff, 1967). In addition, major controversy has been generated by what is called the prevalence of the "medical model" in psychotherapy; this model is said to influence the treating person, the treated person, and society at large.

Psychotherapy has been referred to as an applied field rather than a unique discipline (Ford and Urban, 1963). Bibring (1949) states there is no such thing as psychotherapy, but rather concrete, more or less well-defined methods of psychotherapy. Others suggest that psychotherapy is a specialized set of techniques applicable to specific circumstances and conditions (Strupp, 1973), a set of techniques to alleviate human pain and suffering (Group for the Advancement of Psychiatry, 1978), or a set of structured healing activities performed by a professional who operates in terms of a well-defined rationale shared by therapist and patient (Frank, 1979).

Despite differences there are common themes. The repetitive variables include the concept of psychotherapy as a treatment of psychological disorders (psychic disturbances and mental distress) or problems of coping with life (personal discomfort or maladaptation affecting the self or others). The goals of therapy tend to focus on improvement in functioning (adaptation, feelings, psychic balance) and morale building or support. The methods involve psychological processes or techniques, all of which rely upon the relationship between a trained professional and the person who is in discomfort or who is viewed as having maladaptive or pathological behavior.

Emotional components are usually perceived as inherent to the process, giving it coherence and affecting goals and roles. Garrett (1949) notes that psychotherapy takes into account the client's feelings and emotions and attempts to modify them in a way acceptable to the therapist and client. Frank (1979) considers psychotherapy a major effort to recapture a sense of meaning and significance and affirmation of the self. Ford and Urban (1963, p. 17) call psychotherapy "a procedure wherein two persons engage in a prolonged series of emotion-rousing interactions, mediated primarily by verbal exchanges, the purpose of which is to produce changes in the behavior of one of the pair."

There is recognition that the psychotherapist is equally influenced by emotional (and sometimes irrational) forces. As early as 1910, Freud noted that feelings are aroused in the therapist as a result of the patient's influence on the therapist's unconscious feelings; he called this countertransference. Epstein and Feiner (1979) attribute the increasing emphasis upon and development of theories of countertransference to changing social attitudes toward authority, and also to the humanization of the therapist by such theorists as Sullivan, Fromm, and Fromm-Reichmann. The therapist, however, is not accorded the same freedom as the client to act upon these feelings within the therapeutic relationship. Professional responsibility, training, and ethics dictate the client's needs as being central to the process. As a result, the professional's emotions are of importance only as they clarify the unconscious communication from the client and may be used only for client need. When these feelings express therapist need, they are considered antitherapeutic.

The relationship is most commonly described as professional.

Strean (1978) calls it a controlled relationship addressed exclusively to the internal life of the client. Hamilton (1947, p. 16) notes that psychotherapy is rooted in a two-person relationship; the therapist and the patient or client: "Therapy is a controlled, not a controlling process." It aims to make the client more self-aware and self-directing. Austin (1949) says that psychotherapy that is based on a diagnosis of the total personality takes place in the relationship between two people with the design of bringing about some modification of behavior and attitudes. It has been called an interactive process between two people that addresses itself to the inner difficulties that interfere with an individual's ability to cope with tasks and stresses inherent in human life (Bruch, 1974).

Others refer to it as an educational process (Strupp, Fox, and Lessler 1969). It involves a learning and relearning in which the individual learns new habits and gains new insights (Group for the Advancement of Psychiatry, 1978). Leifer (1969) believes many methods of psychotherapy are really education in personal biography with individuals learning how they are shaped by the society in which they live.

It is always assumed that one of the people is "qualified" or "trained" for the particular process and that the other seeks or is offered help and consciously involves himself or herself in the process. Lack of conscious motivation is considered a deterrent to the process although unconscious resistance is accepted as normal. As a result, psychotherapy is rarely considered possible in authoritarian settings. The professional's understanding, respect, interest, encouragement, and acceptance contribute to client improvement and utilization of the relationship.

THE MEDICAL MODEL

Differences about models of treatment have generated controversies beyond the therapeutic community and professional groups. There is criticism of the medical model and its influence that result in a "sickness" focus for psychotherapy. It is seen as affecting the process, the role of the therapist, the professional affiliation, and "patient" access. Some of the controversy centers on whether or not psychotherapy is a medical procedure.

Coleman (1949) states that *any interviewing* procedure carried out by a psychiatrist is psychotherapy, but another opinion states that psychotherapy consists of any considered and competent *medical endeavor* directed toward the improvement of the emotional health of the individual (Deutsch, 1949). Thus this would seem to include a variety of somatic treatments under the rubric of psychotherapy.

If this term means simply the treatment of psychic disorders there is nothing to argue about. Hitting the patient on the head with a hammer or drenching him with a pail of iced water (generally, the maiden aunts of modern shock therapy) would then pass as psychotherapy. If, however, the term psychotherapy means treating mental disorders by psychological devices, the fact must be faced that apart from one revolutionary development now about 75 years old [Freud's work], nothing psychologically new or advanced has been promoted.

London (1964) emphasizes that the psychotherapist treats no medical illness per se; the methods of psychotherapy have little similarity to medical treatment. There are neither needles nor pins, no bandages and no invasion of the body by a foreign substance, and no malfunctioning of specific organs. The Group for the Advancement of Psychiatry (1978, p. 13) differentiates psychotherapy from other medical treatment:

The patient's so-called "disease" can usually *not* be demonstrated by laboratory, X-ray or "objective" physical findings. This difference makes it essential to clarify the humanitarian, distributive social justice, and cost-benefit issues that relate this form of treatment to the rest of medicine.

Goldberg (1980) clarifies the difference between that which is therapeutic and psychotherapy. He agrees that all somatic treatment such as drugs, hospitalization and some other treatment may be therapeutic, but he states that they do not qualify as psychotherapy—which he defines as any *psychological* intervention designed to alleviate emotional difficulties.

For others, the vocabulary of health and illness, of diagnosis and healing, is considered both narrow and misleading (Leifer, 1969); Szasz (1961) states that mental illness or psychopathology is a myth. The designation of behavior as healthy and normal or sick and abnormal, involves social judgment; certain behaviors, perceived as socially inappropriate, are then integrated into a medical or psychiatric model as illness (Slaby and Tancredi, 1975). Brown (1977) questions the appropriateness of a disease conceptualization of mental and emotional disorders when the locus of care has moved from the hospital—that is, from a clear medical setting—to the community. He suggests that the medical model has doubtful validity in community-based programs that emphasize primary prevention within a social context.

Even the Group for the Advancement of Psychiatry (1978), reviewing the history of the treatment of mental illness, states:

Development of existing bio-medical models of illness, being entirely biochemically orientated, was incapable of including psychological or social factors in the genesis of disease (p. 14).

There is a growing acknowledgement of the role of social variables in the formation and perpetuation of personal, psychological difficulties. Theoretically this is demonstrated through the effect of stress on human behavior (Selye, 1956). The President's Commission on Mental Health (1978) has stated that poverty, unemployment, and discrimination are incriminated in the production of psychological problems. In a criticism of this report Schorr (1979) notes that although there had been movement from talk of mental illness to concern with mental health, the former was still the model because the Commission had continued to be concerned with treatment of disease instead of treatment of cause. Simultaneously, then, the medical model was rejected for causative reasons and accepted for curative ones.

Ahmed, Kolker, and Coelho (1979) believe that because of recent developments in medicine, mental health, and the social sciences, concepts of "disease" and "health" can no longer be defined in purely medical terms. The overwhelming focus of medicine and psychiatry on disease has straitjacketed society's approach to the pursuit of health. The result has been to exclude cultural variations and environmental and psychosocial dimensions from analysis. Because of this, the promotion of health through environmental and social preventive measures and the integrated treatment of the whole person has been neglected.

Robitscher (1979) says that physicians are in the enviable position of setting up classifications that are accepted as such because the physicians have set them up, and of having recognized as diseases whatever they declare to be diseases. This is a mixed blessing, as he notes (p. 217):

Psychiatrists know that many people who consult them are much less "sick" than many or most of the general population. If these patients had decided not to be "patients" but "clients" or "parishioners" and had taken their problems to a social worker, a pastoral counselor, or a faith healer, they would not have incurred appreciable stigma. Their problems in living would not have been defined as medical and there would be no "illness" on their record.

It has been suggested that psychiatry should be used for patients with psychopathology as opposed to those who are merely upset by the vicissitudes of life. Frank (1979, p. 406) introduces an *economic* reason for not doing so:

Unfortunately, psychopathology cannot be sharply distinguished from other manifestations of distress, and if troubled people were to be excluded from our offices, there would be very little left of our practice.

Another psychiatrist, Gordon (1979, p. 416), applauds a new approach in mental health services in which:

Disease is seen as the result of an imbalance among a variety of social, personal and economic as well as biological influences and healing as a method for restoring balance within the individual and between the individual and the environment.

He stresses the need to address the whole person in a total enviroment.

The social work perspective has been more uniform and consistent. Hollis (1980) has said that few social workers have ever denied the importance of either the person or the environment. One of the distinguishing features of the profession from the beginning has been the central theme of these two aspects of life–the psychological and the social. More than 30 years ago Coleman (1949) remarked that in the area of relations of the person to a situation of stress or distress social workers have acquired a certainty, a skill, and a professional maturity that is not found in any other profession. In fact, from the initial involvement with those who needed "charity" it became very clear to the profession that social, economic, and other deprivations influenced, developed, and exacerbated physical, mental, and emotional difficulties. However, even in social work there has been continuing discussions about the medical/nonmedical model, and the relative emphasis put upon personality and social variables. Simon (1977, p. 386) thought it necessary to say the following:

It has been pointed out repeatedly that the assaults of the environment have emotional and psychological impact on the individual's view of the external world and of himself and can affect his behavior in the environment. To take serious account of this impact is to give attention to the realities of the human condition. Serious attention to the personally internalized effects of environmental and social deprivation does not constitute a "disease model" or a psychopathological orientation for social work. It means, simply, that the social work profession must accept and develop further the central element of its historical function which is individualization.

Social work has always stressed a series of values that stem from the interdependence of the person and society. It values the meeting of human needs. Its tradition has been to provide those services that promote, restore, maintain, or enhance the functioning of individuals, singly or in families and groups, and, as well, those services that might prevent dysfunction. Although this may lead to involvement with the planning, developing, and implementing of social policies in relation to services for people, social work has never taken upon itself the role of changing society. Its historic role has been the delivery of service.

The profession charges society with the responsibility of meeting the needs of its members. These include more than those basic for human survival. Human beings need to be respected and to be valued because of their individual worth and inherent dignity. From this flows the right to privacy and confidentiality, the right to share in resources, and the right of all individuals to determine the course of their lives as long as this does not interfere with the similar rights of others.

Early in this century Mary Richmond (1917) noted that the client's own hopes, plans, and attitudes toward life are more important than any single item of information; she stressed the importance of the family, but noted that a client's social relations are not bounded by the immediate family. She amplified this perspective a few years later (1922) by saying that the development of personality is central to the tradition of casework. She identified the client–worker relationship as an important tool, and said that the art of social casework is discovering and assuring to the individual the best possible social relatedness. She explained that this work consists of "processes which develop personality through adjustments consciously affected, individual by individual, between men and their social environment" (pp. 98–99). The worker is no more occupied with abnormalities in the individual than in the environment, nor able to neglect one or the other.

THE PROFESSIONAL

The controversy about the medical model is heightened by competition among the various professional groups for recognition as providers of psychotherapy. London (1964, p. 152) notes that:

For some years now, psychotherapists in this country have been seeking the passage of legislation that will either incorporate psychotherapy under existing Medical Practices Acts, in the case of psychiatrists, or that will license or certify psychologists. The efforts of each professional group are partly attempts to gain competitive advantage over the other, and the area of almost complete professional overlap, therefore of competition, is psychotherapy. Some psychiatrists would like to obtain a monopoly on the psychotherapy business by having it declared a branch of medicine, thus squeezing out the psychologists who, for the most part, engage in the same business but are not physicians. Some psychologists would like to improve their competitive position vis-à-vis psychiatrists by having themselves legally sanctioned, either as practitioners of psychotherapy (licenses), or at least as a specialized profession to which there is only limited access (certification).

In the two decades that have passed since that statement, the competition has become more intense because of the growth of a variety of insurance plans, and the development of "community psychiatry," outreach programs, and government payment for services to those who cannot pay for themselves.

London disposes of social work's position in this matter, simply and incorrectly. Stating that social workers do more psychotherapy than psychiatrists and psychologists together, but do not participate in this debate, he advances two reasons (p. 152):

1. The issues mostly affect private practice, and few social workers are in private practice.

2. Social work is traditionally the handmaiden of psychiatry, and most social workers are content to function under the supervision of psychiatrists. They had as well be, for membership in the National Association of Social Workers apparently demands that any clinics in which they work be directed by psychiatrists.

London seems to have read little of the social work literature. Indeed, social work has a historic interest in psychotherapy and has been involved in the struggle for recognition and for independent practice. As early as 1918 issues relating to autonomy and identity were addressed by Mary Jarrett, when she spoke to the first class at the Smith School of Social Work (Reynolds, 1963, p. 62).

...our new discipline, psychiatric social work, holds two possibilities; we could think of ourselves as assistants in psychotherapy, working under the direction of psychiatrists...or we could develop a profession in our own right, bringing to psychotherapy the social outlook and skills which would require our thinking for ourselves and would place us alongside psychiatrists as another but different allied professional.

Over the years social work has struggled with the problem of independence from supervision by a member of another profession (often mandated by laws, regulations, or financing policies), with the right of social workers to practice autonomously, and to be in the private practice of psychotherapy. Garrett (1949) noted that caseworkers absorb, synthesize, and apply knowledge from many fields, psychoanalytic, medical, sociological, psychological, and cultural. This knowledge is applied for their own professional purposes, using their own professional methods and their own supervision. Noting that some workers were concentrating on selected psychoanalytic skills under analytic supervision for psychotherapy or for lay analysis, she said there was a danger of losing the professional identity or of becoming "the handmaiden of another profession" (p. 225).

In a retrospective work, Helen Harris Perlman (1971, p. x) remarked:

The concern to establish social casework's particular practice area and expertise has been predominant in my professional thinking for a long time. It did not trouble me when I practiced and supervised practice in the two private family agencies that initiated me into social work and provided me over many years with a wide-ranging and rich experience...But uncertainties arose and proliferated as I moved to studentship in a psychiatric hospital where to my wide-eyed amazement I found that not infrequently I knew considerably more about their field than many of the psychiatric residents knew; indeed, the head psychiatrist asked *me*, a student social worker, to teach *them*, student psychiatrists, how to interview for diagnostic and treatment purposes. Then several years later...into a combination of child-guidance/school-social work clinic, I was further unsettled, this time by a...blurring of functions among members of the 'team'.

Social work is the only profession that demands intensive clinical experience for its terminal degree, the M.S.W. The two-year curriculum is required to include a minimum of 1200 hours in direct client service. This is not true of curricula in medicine or psychology. Thus professionals in these disciplines are not prepared after graduation to help people in relation to emotional problems. The practice of psychiatry or clinical psychology necessitates additional training. Despite this, there are some who practice without any basic preparation for these specialities.

Even in social work, the master's degree is not a cheap credential for the practice of psychotherapy. It is considered only the foundation for further study. Chapter 3, "Beyond the Master's Degree: Education for Social Work Psychotherapy," delineates the intensive study and extended experience that are considered necessary.

The settings in which social workers work vary in professional aegis. Many agencies are under social work auspices, but others are under the primary authority of another discipline: in hospitals, medicine; in schools, education. However, even in social agencies the psychiatric consultant frequently has the greatest authority, if only because of government regulations concerning mental health establishments and the requirements for third-party insurance payments. There is an increasing push by psychiatrists to promulgate guidelines and have them adopted by governmental and insurance regulations to ensure that psychiatrists will see and diagnose all patients, formulate treatment plans, refer patients, and review the treatment on a periodic basis (Knoll, 1979). In many states graduate social workers are not yet licensed as independent professionals. As a result, a senior social worker with many years of experience may have to defer to the opinion of a much less experienced psychiatric consultant.

Frank (1979) notes that community mental health centers have aggravated tensions among professionals. With the trend towards third-party payments, there is intensified competition among psychiatrists, psychologists, and social workers.

Each profession seeks to define what it does as reimbursible while excluding members of other professions who do essentially the same thing. Since there is no rational way of resolving this conflict, it is being decided in reality by the relative political power of the different professional organizations. The battle is being waged primarily, therefore, by psychiatrists and psychologists, with the relatively powerless social workers under attack by both (p. 406).

In a similar vein, Leifer (1969) agrees that the main significance of the medical/nonmedical nature of psychotherapy is that it both raises and settles the issue of who should be permitted to practice.

If psychotherapy is a medical activity, then it should be practiced only by physicians. If it is not a medical activity then it may be practiced by qualified psychologists, social workers and other non-medical persons (p. 147).

Yarmolinsky (1978) notes that where questions have arisen as to the boundaries of professional authority, the courts and legislatures have generally reflected the balance of power among competing professions.

Some major realities are neglected. At present the control of psychotherapy—what it is, how it can be practiced, and by whom—

has become the domain of bureaucrats and insurance companies. All professions lose by turning over such control; all people in need of help with biopsychosocial problems lose. Need, prevention, and understanding become subservient to cost. Present expenditures, with little regard to future consequences, determine the range and extent of service.

The social work professional has special problems. The profession emphasizes and reflects society's most highly developed ideals, strivings, ethics, and values. Towle (1954) and Rapoport (1968) suggest that, by its very nature and function, social work is committed to a group that at times may need to be protected and as often actively defended. The profession developed and continues to exist because the community has had a conscience about its disadvantaged population, even when this disadvantage occurs because of social inequities. Social work has become the embodiment of society's conscience.

Conscience does not lead only to altruism; struggles over the demands of conscience as easily lead to conflict, ambivalence, and anger. As an unwelcome reminder of society's failures, and even though the profession is numerically large and growing, its position vis-à-vis society is similar to that of a minority group. Like other minorities, social work suffers from society's contradictory attitudes toward its purposes and functions. As a result, attacks on the social work profession often occur when society is neglecting those most in need of services. Social work also is accused of being unsuccessful because the profession has not solved long-standing social problems. And ambivalence is generated toward the social work profession because it is one of the articulate forces striving toward planned social change. In another context, speaking of society's responsibility for the development of neurosis, Freud (1910, p. 292) noted:

Just as we make any single person our enemy by discovering what is repressed in him, so the community cannot respond with sympathy to a relentless exposure of its injurious effects and deficiencies.

PEOPLE IN PSYCHOTHERAPY

The appropriate "patient" for psychotherapy has been described as one who is relatively intelligent, capable of fairly rational communication, and strongly dissatisfied with his or her present state of life and determined to improve it (Harper, 1974). A study of the characteristics that enable people to utilize interpersonal help successfully concluded that these include good coping capacity or problem-solving ability, verbal skill, the ability to establiish relationships with others, and emotional responsiveness (Frank et al., 1978). With these characteristics, it is difficult to ascertain the "illness," yet, when people enter psychotherapy, too often they are called and become "patients." In addition to suggesting illness, there are prescriptions for the role of the sick person and the healer as established by the culture (Parsons, 1951a, b).

Different cultural beliefs and backgrounds have been noted as determining attitudes toward mental and physical illness. For many, physical illness is preferred and understood, whereas mental or emotional disturbance is incomprehensible (Kleinman, 1979). The emotional origin of many physical complaints has been noted in large populations (Strole et al., 1962). When sickness is accepted as the model by the person in psychotherapy, expectations for self-activity and doctor activity may deviate considerably from those that are considered necessary for the process of psychotherapy, unless the therapy stresses the goal—to feel better and to have less discomfort—rather than a focus on disturbance or illness.

Austin (1949) suggests that different disciplines often have different patients–clients. People whose major complaints are concern with symptoms tend to go to psychiatrists (or be referred there). Those who suffer with breakdowns in social relationships, marital relationships, work adjustment, and parent–child relationships, and who have some awareness of psychological components, may seek help from either psychiatry or social work. But those who project their inner problems on social difficulties, and who act out their problems, will more often find their way to the social agency. Today these people are also seen in community mental health settings.

This last group does not have the characteristics generally considered necessary for psychotherapy. Generally, client groups who somatize, those who are uneducated, and most often those who are poor, are also considered unsuitable. Very poor people have often been labeled as unable to communicate, particularly with middle class professionals. In addition, a large number are experienced by professionals as "repulsive" (Lieberman and Gottesfeld, 1973). They are then rejected by professionals, who tend to view them as ineligible for insight therapy and resistant to psychotherapeutic intervention. Such judgments are "the result of the therapist's disability rather than the client's inability to be helped" (p. 22).

There seem to be two kinds of people in need of help: those who are desirable candidates for psychotherapy and those who are not. The undesirables are too often medicated, subjected to a five- or ten-minute hour, or sent to the least desired psychiatric settings, such as state hospitals. It is as if the psychiatric community is unwilling to treat them; this is left for social work.

SOCIAL WORK PSYCHOTHERAPY

Littner (1971) has noted that social workers have more training and intensive experience with individuals or families who have many difficulties and with those who are "hard to reach" than any other professional group. This is also true for clients who are poor, deprived, less educated, less intellectual, and often action-oriented. It includes working class clients, and others, regardless of socioeconomic class, who have problems in social relationships and difficulties in emotional responsiveness.

The ethics and values of the profession demand that the client be offered service according to need. "Starting where the client is" acknowledges that treatment depends "on what the client is willing to accept and participate in" (Hollis, 1964, p. 204). It suggests that the client's need should be met by the form of treatment that will bring the greatest relief and forward movement. In addition, agency and worker must be sufficiently flexible to adapt to the varying needs of diverse population groups.

What social workers attempt to do has been called "psychotherapy plus" (Strean, 1978). In addition to addressing the internal life of the client, attention is always directed toward the interactions and transactions within the social orbit. Clients' maladaptive behaviors, as well as malignant elements within the client's environments, become targets for modification, as indicated. "The client is always—and implicitly—a social complex, because he/she is social, and also a psychological one since the one is a concurrent function of the other" (Falck, 1978, p. 42).

The concept of the psychosocial viewpoint in social work was originally used to convey a bridge between psychological and sociological theories (Hollis, 1964). Today it conveys a distinct orientation to psychotherapy and it is being adopted by other professionals

(Turner, 1978). The social nature of social work psychotherapy is stressed in the preferred term "client," although in many interdisciplinary settings and in communications with other professions this term may be difficult to use and not always understood. On the other hand, acceptance of the terms psychotherapy, therapy, and therapist are not suggesting acceptance of assumptions of disease or pathology. They are used to imply accountability, responsibility, training, and social authentication (Turner, 1978).

Social work psychotherapy has the objective of bringing about that change in behaviors that will improve individual functioning and the relationship between individuals and their social environment. To achieve this objective people are understood and treated differentially in relation to social problems as well as to intrapsychic problems, which are perceived as interrelated. This is the social work identity and history.

The provision of varied services, which include psychotherapy, is also an integral aspect of the identity and history of social work. Thus it is not surprising that social workers are responsible for the delivery of clinical service that exceeds the total of all of the other helping professions combined. Unfortunately, pressured working conditions provide the least amount of time for clinical writing, a medium for advertising knowledge and skill. However, social work clinicians understand the need to make time for this activity as evidenced in the success of the *Clinical Social Work Journal* and a slow but steady production of books by social workers about psychotherapy. This book is one in that development.

REFERENCES

Ahmed, P. I., Kolker, A. and Coelho, G. V. Toward a New Definition of Health: An Overview. In P. I. Ahmed and G. V. Coelho (Eds.) *Toward a New Definition of Health*. New York: Plenum Press, 1979.

Austin, L. Trends in Differential Treatment in Casework. In *Proceedings of National Conference of Social Work 1948*. New York: Columbia Universiy Press, 1949.

Bergin, A. E. and Strupp, H. H. *Changing Frontiers in the Science of Psychotherapy*. New York: Aldine, Atherton, 1972.

Bibring, E. Condensation of the Discussion: From Report of the Symposium on Psychotherapy and Casework of the Boston Psychoanalytic Society and Institute, Inc. *Social Casework*, 1949, 30, 252.

Blanck, R. The Case for Casework. *Smith College Sudies in Social Work*, 1979, 49, 192–208.

Brown, B. S. Conflict and Detente Between Social Issues and Clinical Practice. *American Journal of Orthopsychiatry*, 1977, 47:3, 466–475.

Bruch, H. *Learning Psychotherapy*. Cambridge, Mass.: Harvard University Press, 1974.

Coleman, J. V. Distinguishing Between Psychotherapy and Casework. *Social Casework*, 1949, 30: 244–251.

Deutsch, L. Condensation of the Discussion: From Report of the Program of the Symposium on Psychotherapy and Casework of the Boston Psychoanalytic Society and Institute, Inc. *Social Casework*, 1949, 30, 252.

Epstein, L., and Feiner, A. H. (Eds.) *Countertransference*. New York: Jason Aronson, 1979.

Falck, H. S. The Individuality-Groupness Effect: Phenomenology, Social Values and Clinical Applications. *Social Thought*, Summer 1978.

Ford, D. H., and Urban, H. B. *Systems of Psychotherapy*. New York: John Wiley & Sons, 1963.

Frank, J. D. Mental Health in a Fragmented Society: The Shattered Crystal Ball. *American Journal of Orthopsychiatry*, 1979, 49, 394-398.

Frank. J. D. Hoedn-Saric, R., Liberman, B. L., and Stone, A. R. *Effectiveness Ingredients of Successful Psychotherapy*. New York: Brunner/Mazel, 1978.

Freud, S., The Future Prospects of Psychoanalytic Therapy. In *Collected Works II; 1910*, 285–296.

Garrett, A. Historical Survey of the Evolution of Casework. *Social Casework*, 1949, 30, 219–229.

Glover, E., Remarks on Success and Failure in Psychoanalysis and Psychotherapy, in B. B. Wolman (Ed.) *Success and Failure in Psychoanalysis and Psychotherapy*, New York: Macmillan, 1972.

Goldberg, A., Self-Psychology and the Distinctiveness of Psychotherapy. in R. Langs (Ed.) *International Journal of Psychoanalytic Psychotherapy*. New York: Jason Aronson, 1980.

Gordon, J. S. Mental Health Services: Alternatives Now and For the Future. in P. I. Ahmed and G. V. Coelho (Eds.) *Toward a New Definition of Health*, New York: Plenum Press, 1979.

Group for the Advancement of Psychiatry *On Psychotherapy and Casework* No. 71. New York: Group for the Advancement of Psychiatry, 1969.

Group for the Advancement of Psychiatry, *Psychotherapy and Its Financial Feasibility Within The National Health Care System*, vol. X, Publication no. 100. New York: Group for the Advancement of Psychiatry, 1978.

Gunderson, J. G., and Mosher, L. R. (Ed) *Psychotherapy of Shizophrenia*. New York: Jason Aronson, 1975.

Hamilton, G. *Psychotherapy In Child Guidance*. New York: Columbia University Press, 1947.

Harper, R. A. *Psychoanalysis and Psychotherapy*. New York: Jason Aronson, 1974.

Hollis, F. *Casework: A Psychosocial Therapy*. New York: Random House, 1964.

Hollis, F. On Revisiting Social Work. *Social Casework* 1980, 61:1, 3–10.

Kernberg, O. *Internal World and External Reality*, New York: Jason Aronson, 1980.

Kleinman, A. Sickness as Cultural Semantics: Issues for an Anthropological Medical and Psychiatry. In P. I. Ahmed and G. V. Coelho (Eds.) *Toward a New Definition of Mental Health*. New York: Plenum Press, 1979.

Knoll, D. Psychiatric Supervision for Social Work? *Clinical Social Work Journal*, 1979, 7:3, 214–217.

Leifer, R. *In The Name Of Mental Health*. New York: Science House, 1969.

Lieberman, F., and Gottesfeld, M. The Repulsive Client. *Clinical Social Work Journal*, 1973, 1:1, 22–31.

Liem, J. H. Family Studies of Schizophrenia: An Update and Commentary. *Schizophrenia Bulletin*, 1980, 6:3, 429–455.

Littner, N. Special Problems of Training Psychotherapists To Work With Children. In R. R. Holt (Ed.) *New Horizon for Psychotherapy*. New York: International Universities Press, 1971.

London, P. *The Modes and Morals of Psychotherapy*. New York: Holt, Rinehart and Winston, 1964.

Marmor, J. Current Trends in Psychotherapy. In H. Davanloo (Ed.) *Short-Term Dynamic Psychotherapy*. New York and London: S. P. Medical and Scientific Books, 1978.

Marshall, E. Psychotherapy Faces Test of Worth. *Science*, January 1980, 207, 35–36. (a)

Marshall, E. Psychotherapy Works, But For Whom? *Science*, February 1980, 207. (b)

Parsons, T. *The Social System*. Glencoe, Ill. The Free Press of Glencoe, 1951.(a)

Parsons, T. Illness and the Role of the Physician: A Sociological Perspective. *American Journal of Orthopsychiatry*. 21: 1951, 452–560. (b)

Perlman, H. H. *Perspectives On Social Casework*. Philadelphia. Temple University Press, 1971.

Pinkus, H., et al. Education for the Practice Of Clinical Social Work at the Master's Level: A Position Paper. *Clinical Social Work Journal*, 1977, 5(4), 253–268.

The President's Commission on Mental Health *Report of The President, 1978*. Washington, D. C., U. S. Government Printing Office.

Rapaport, L. Creativity in Social Work. *Smith College Studies In Social Work*, 1968, 38:3, 139.

Reynolds, B., *An Uncharted Journey: Fifty Years of Growth In Social Work*. New York: Citadel Press, 1963.

Richmond, M. *Social Diagnosis*. New York: Russell Sage Foundation, 1917.

Richmond, M. *What Is Social Casework*. New York: Russell Sage Foundation, 1922.

Robitscher, J. Labeling and Discrimination in Mental Health. In P. I. Ahmed and G. V. Coelho (Eds.) *Toward a New Definition of Health*. New York: Plenum Press, 1979.

Schorr, A. L. The President's Commission on Mental Health as a Symptom. *American Journal of Orthopsychiatry*, 1979, 49.8, 388–391.

Selye, H. *The Stress of Life*. New York: McGraw-Hill, 1956.

Simon, B. K. Diversity and Unity in the Social Work Profession. *Social Work*, 1977, 22:5, 394–400.

Slaby, F., and Tancredi, L. *Collusion for Conformity*. New York: Jason Aronson,. 1975.

Slovenko, R. Psychotherapy and Informed Consent: A Search in Judicial

Regulation. In W. E. Barton and C. J. Sanborn (Eds.) *Law and The Mental Health Professions*. New York: International Universities Press, 1978.

Strean, H.S. *Clinical Social Work Theory And Practice*. New York: Free Press, 1978.

Strole, L., et al. *Mental Health in the Metropolis*. New York: Harper & Row, 1962.

Strupp, H. H. *Psychotherapy: Clinical, Research and Theoretical Issues*. New York: Jason Aronson, 1973.

Strupp, H. H., Fox, R. E., and Lessler, K. *Patients View Their Psychotherapy*. Baltimore and London; The John Hopkins Press, 1969.

Szasz, T. *The Myth of Mental Illness: Foundations of a Theory of Personal Conduct*. New York: Hoeber, 1961.

Towle, C. *The Learner in Education for the Professions*. Chicago: University of Chicago Press, 1954.

Truax, C. B., and Carkhuff, R. R. *Toward Effective Counseling and Psychotherapy: Training and Practice*. Chicago: Aldine-Atherton, 1967.

Turner, F. J. *Psychosocial Therapy*. New York: Free Press, 1978.

Wolberg, L. *The Technique of Psychotherapy*. New York: Grune & Stratton, 1977.

Yarmolinsky, A. The Professional in American Society. *Daedalus*. 1978, 107:1.

MARCELLA BAIRD

2

Social Work Contributions to Psychotherapy

EACH OF THE PROFESSIONS engaged in psychotherapy has developed a distinctive model and style of practice growing out of its historic origin and mission and the characteristics of its value orientation. Knowledge, methods, and techniques produced by each discipline have been shared, either purposefully or serendipitously, with the others. Social work has made many such contributions. These need to be affirmed at this time because there is insufficient recognition of those aspects of psychotherapy that have their roots in the social work orientation and knowledge base. Indeed, there is so little awareness of these contributions that the other professions, in some parts of the United States, have lobbied to have laws enacted that prohibit social workers from referring to any part of their practice as psychotherapy.

It has not always been so. There is sufficient evidence in the literature reflecting the effort made by both social work and psychiatry to examine the way in which the two professions practice psychotherapy. Social work theoreticians, Hollis (1949, 1964, 1960), Austin (1956) and Hamilton (1940, 1949), were clear that social workers engage in psychotherapy. The Group for the Advancement of Psychiatry (1969) concluded that social workers practice psychotherapy in many settings. Coleman (1949), at a symposium on psychia-

---

A revised version of a paper originally presented at the Menninger Foundation, 1975.

try and casework sponsored by the Boston Psychoanalytic Society, although drawing distinct differences between casework treatment and psychotherapy as practiced by psychiatrists, stated unequivocally, "While casework has learned a great deal from the dynamic understanding and therapeutic orientation of psychiatry, it has also returned a great deal to psychiatry, and many of the techniques used in psychotherapy show the influence of casework thinking." (p.251)

PERSON-IN-SITUATION

From its earliest days in the latter part of the 19th century, social casework has had a commitment to the application of a scientific method of helping people. Mary Richmond, the profession's first theorist, enunciated her definition of social casework in 1922 and established the basic position of the profession that still distinguishes social work from all the other helping professions (Richmond, 1922). This definition, which states that "social casework consists of those processes which develop personality through adjustments consciously effected, individual by individual between men and their social environment" (p. 98) is commonly abbreviated to "the person in his/her situation." This implies there is a need for three kinds of knowledge: knowledge of the personality—a psychophysiological system and its components and development, both normal and abnormal; knowledge of the social environment in all of its ramifications as a social system with cultural, racial, ethnic, and economic realities; and knowledge and understanding of how the two (person and situation) impinge on and interact with one another.

Accepting the tripartite complex person-in-situation demands the development of skills in diagnosing all components of the systems to determine where dysfunction is occurring and, equally important, where the strength lies to be utilized in overcoming the dysfunction. It further demands the development of skill in helping clients to struggle successfully, not only within themselves and within their complicated interpersonal relationships, but also with the sometimes formidable social, legal, educational, and financial institutions with which they may be in difficulty. This ability to intervene constructively in the client's real world is a valuable tool in psychotherapy, as is the ability to determine when to encourage the client to take an action on his or her own behalf. This tool is less often used by other professional disciplines. Indeed, the Committee on Psychiatry and the Community of the Group for the Advancement of Psychiatry (1975) has noted:

Although medical students and psychiatric residents are often exposed to poor patients, they seldom have contact with their patient's families and almost never make home visits, and the task of investigating the social and financial conditions of their patients is usually delegated to the social worker. The student and resident thus lose an important opportunity to become familiar with a critically important part of their patients' real world, and to discover for themselves how they might make effective contributions to mental health through the welfare system (p. 462).

Case illustration 1

In a general hospital outpatient psychiatric clinic, two psychiatrists were discussing a woman who had just been seen by the resident. She was a Medicaid recipient, single, middle-aged, drab and inarticulate. Her complaint was exhaustion resulting from her inability to sleep because she was fearful of fire. Her request was for sleeping medication. The psychiatrists were discussing the meaning of the symptom in terms of phobia and anxiety hysteria, and were considering whether to use medication alone or to combine it with psychotherapy. In view of her verbal limitations, the usefulness of psychotherapy was in question. The social worker was asked for her opinion; she asked them instead if they knew where the woman lived. A glance at the application revealed she was one of the occupants of a notorious tenement building that had had several fires during the past few weeks and that was now being considered for condemnation. With this new information, the diagnosis was changed to situational reaction, no medication was prescribed, and no psychotherapy was initiated. Instead, the woman's sleeplessness was explained to her as an appropriate response to a dangerous situation, her fear as highly realistic. It was suggested she visit friends in a safer location so she could sleep and then make plans to move. She was also referred to a social agency that might assist her in finding a suitable apartment within her ability to pay for it. (This usefulness of the social work approach was recognized very early in the 20th century. Richard C. Cabot, a physician, added social workers to The Massachusetts General Hospital staff in 1905 because he understood that it was necessary for a complete diagnosis to include information about home, diet, work, family relationships, and problems.)

SELF-DETERMINATION

Differences in value orientations lead to differences in style of working. Social workers believe in the client's "right to self-determination." The use of the term "client," implying an equality of position, a sharing in a joint enterprise, is indicative of this attitude. As Coleman (1949) said: "The social worker's goal [of helping the client to deal with his situational problems] actually involves a much more far-reaching respect of person than is found in the practice of psychiatry, or for that matter, of medicine. The case worker respects the consciously expressed wishes of the client though offering help towards clarifying those wishes, whereas the psychiatrist, at least in his philosophic orientation, accepts no such limitation" (pp. 247–248). This is a recognition of the social work intent to keep the clients' reasons for seeking help primary and to assist in achieving the goals to which they aspire. In the course of working toward those goals, the social worker may help clients become aware of how they hinder themselves. There then may be an implicit agreement to work toward improvement in their functioning as another goal. Actually, sometimes the best service the worker can provide clients is to help them find goals for themselves (Perlman, 1970). With lost and alienated youth this has become an important segment of the practice of many psychotherapists of all disciplines during the past two decades. Perhaps it has been forgotten that at one time it was considered appropriate for the therapist to prescribe for patients how they should live and, therefore, to arrange psychotherapy in such a way that clients would realize not their own goals, but rather their therapist's goals for them. (Some feminists still warn women to beware of this possibility when they seek therapy.) To the extent that this is no longer true, it appears that the social work value orientation has been incorporated into the general practice of psychotherapy.

NURTURANCE

Social work is often referred to as "social service," a reflection on the nurturing aspect of the profession and its commitment to members of society who suffer social and economic deprivation. Social workers are familiar with dependency and expect to encounter it regularly. They meet it on the assumption that it is natural for unmet dependency to produce helplessness, resentment, anxiety, and confusion, which in turn foster further dependency and social incompetence (Towle, 1945, 1948). Another way to consider the meeting of normal dependency is to refer to it as the establishment of a positive transference to assist in the therapeutic work and to prevent the creation of barriers. This is not to say that pathological dependency is catered to or that negative transference is ignored. However, social workers understand that what may sometimes be thought to be negative transference may be the result of the therapist's refusal to meet the normal dependency needs of the client due to the mistaken belief that such action fosters dependence. The social worker who enables a good and positive relationship through meeting natural need has the freedom to challenge characteristic maladaptive defenses quite early and consistently without threatening the relationship. On the other hand, during the therapeutic work the client will be helped to engage identifiable strengths to master problems. This is done in preference to emphasizing pathology and in the service of diminishing its importance in the client's life, thus changing the self-image and fostering ego growth. This emphasis has gained for social work its reputation for skill in supportive psychotherapy with psychotic people, although it is by no means used only with them. Sometimes the social worker might elect to enlarge the client's repertoire of coping skills by modeling appropriate problem-solving behavior for that client (Bandler, 1961; McBroom, 1970), even as simultaneously, there is attention to less conscious material. For instance, several sessions might include teaching a client job-hunting skills and role-playing interviews, and at the same time engaging in discussions about attitudes toward authority and relationships with parents and other authority figures.

REALITY AND TRANSFERENCE

Whereas psychotherapists from another discipline often ignore the realities in their clients' lives or treat them as metaphors for what is going on within the therapeutic relationship, social workers will focus sharply on specific issues which are problematic for their clients such as current intra- or interpersonal conflicts. This approach has long been a recognized contribution. A clients' attention will be directed to the transferences established toward the significant people in his or her life, which will be interpreted as they are reported to the social worker.

Another stylistic difference which increases interventive options that social workers employ is to utilize the transferences to themselves as metaphors for what is going on between clients and the significant people in their lives. This will keep the treatment highly relevant to the clients' lives while removing the mystique of treatment, especially in early meetings.

Case Illustration 2

A sallow, somber nurse in her 30s requested help in examining her unsatisfying marriage to an alcoholic, despotic husband. She had come at the urging of a friend who had watched her descend into near-apathy. She worked on the night shift at a nearby hospital and came for therapy on the way home in the morning. Mrs. O. experienced no joy in living, feeling she had "jumped from the frying pan into the fire" by marrying in order to escape from her controlling, domineering father, in whose restaurant she had worked while attending nursing school prior to her marriage. She felt that no matter how she tried, she could please no one, and that there was no energy or time left over from work at home and at the hospital for any enjoyment. "My life has always been a grey place." Her affect was flat. Her tone was resigned. She had apparently been in a low-grade depression for a long time.

Despite her stated concern about her marriage, Mrs. O. usually chose to talk about her job, especially her relationship with her immediate superior, a nun, whom she characterized as a severe, critical, grudging woman. The social worker (a woman) began to serve coffee and doughnuts during their sessions. Soon Mrs. O. seemed to be more lively and smiling, but her bitter complaints about her supervisor continued.

However, one morning she expressed confusion. As she accepted her coffee, she commented that the supervisor had invited her to have coffee with her. She had become quite nervous, had fixed a cup for the supervisor, and said she had to work. But the supervisor insisted she sit down and relax and not work so hard. She had sat down, "What else could I do? But I still wonder what she's up to." The worker challenged her suspiciousness and wondered in her turn if Mrs. O. had similar suspicions of her. After all, she, too, offered coffee.

There ensued an examination of Mrs. O.'s expectations of a "boss" and a more searching evaluation of the nun, which cast doubt on Mrs. O.'s negative impression of her. During the next few weeks Mrs. O. reported more positive experiences at work. She began to wear lipstick. The worker finally expressed reservations about Mrs. O.'s understanding of her relationship to her supervisor, pointing to discrepancies between the factual accounts of their interactions and her interpretations of them. Gradually she began to recognize how she projected her exaggerated expectations of herself onto her supervisor because she expected all bosses to be like the father who was so demanding of her. As her anxiety at work subsided and she began to allow herself to enjoy the supervisor's approval that she could now no longer refuse to trust, her attention turned toward examining her relationship with her father, who was a harsh and cruel man, still powerful in her life. In this process she also talked about her husband, recognizing that she had cast him in a villain's role, as she had the supervisor. She could see that he was actually a rather ineffectual person who despised himself because he was unable to support the family on his earnings, so that, despite his dislike of it, she had to work. She thought that his self-depreciation might be contributing to his need to drink excessively. She remembered she had chosen to marry him because he was so unlike her father. "And I've been painting him the same and making us all miserable."

During the last few sessions Mrs. O. began wearing an attracive new hairstyle and a new coral-colored coat, in place of her old olive-green one. She was cheerful and optimistic; she seemed to enjoy her job and saw her husband's willingness to attend AA meetings as offering the possibility of more satisfaction in her marriage. She felt better about her relationship with her father as she no longer carried so great a burden of guilt for her anger and antagonism toward him, feeling now that "he worked for it and deserves it." In reviewing her experience in therapy, she commented that she had realized the very first time she had come that "something good would happen here" because, when she arrived, the worker had picked up her old green coat and hung it up on the rack, "as though it mattered, like a good coat." Her husband had been sneering at the coat, telling her to "get rid of that rag." She had felt he really meant her and not the coat. But now she was glad to have tossed it out. "It's not good enough to give to anyone else and I don't need it any more."

Here we see how a respectful acceptance of the client's dependency with appropriately timed nurturing responses creates the positive therapeutic climate that permits highly focused treatment. Mrs. O. also demonstrates the client's heightened sensitivity to the therapist's many small gestures of courtesy or disdain which take on symbolic meanings,, whether experienced by the client as transference phenomena or as realities. The conscious, disciplined use of self as a real person is considered by social workers to be the most potent tool in providing a therapeutic relationship. Transference phenomena will emerge regardless, and because the worker is well known by the client, the irrationality of these phenomena can be more easily experienced. Thus Mrs. O. could readily evaluate her suspiciousness of the supervisor and the worker for being kind to her when it was called to her attention. We might also wonder what might have happened in this therapeutic encounter had the therapist ignored the fallen coat or had Mrs. O. experienced her hanging it up as a gesture of criticism for her carelessness.

Case Illustration 3

Mrs. T., a chic, pretty, 33-year-old wife of an executive and mother of three small boys (ages 5 through 8) had been seen several times before appearing one day with her youngest son, supposedly because her baby sitter had been unavailable. She seemed unable to disengage herself from the boy, although she pleaded with him to let her go into the social worker's office without him. Her voice became more and more whiney and she looked increasingly anxious, as did the boy, who refused to remain in the waiting room. The social worker firmly announced that there was no further time for discussion. The boy was to stay and play in the waiting room and his mother was to come into the office, which adjoined the waiting room. Further, the boy was not to call to her or to knock on the door. When the mother had finished, she would emerge.

Once in the office with the door shut, Mrs. T. expressed admiration of the worker's expeditious handling of the child. She revealed that she was never in control of any situation with her children. She begged and wheedled, but they paid no attention. It had never occurred to her to do as the worker had done: to tell them what to do and to expect obedience. She then described a chaotic childhood in a primitive Appalachian cabin with a pair of ineffectual nonparenting parents from whom she had learned how to fight with her husband in exotic ways, but not how to run an organized household or care for her children. This client had not explicitly requested help in developing parenting skills. She had come to the family agency ostensibly to "work out in my mind" whether she wanted to continue her unsatisfying marriage. Had the worker ignored the implicit demand for help which the demonstration of ineptitude represented, or had she turned the session immediately following into an educational one on child rearing, or sent her to another facility for parenting education, the client's dependence would have been unmet and she might have had her feelings of worthlessness reified.

Instead, the worker led her into an examination of her recognition that she had learned a marital style from her parents. She mischievously described her last "bad fight" with her husband, when she had dumped a basket of six new kittens on him as he lay in bed and then had gone storming off to the children's room to spend the rest of the night with them, as she usually did when angry with him. She looked quite uncomfortable and admitted to shame and guilt for using the boys to make her husband jealous, but also defiantly said she couldn't help behaving this way. "It's all I know."

In the next hour Mrs T. was quite subdued. She first shyly described her attempts to act like a mother and to be in charge during the past week, but soon fell into silence. With encouragement to speak, she burst into tears, saying that since the last session she had been preoccupied with specific, acutely disturbing memories. She wanted help with them, but was ashamed to reveal them. Finally, with sobs and tears she described her parents' nocturnal quarrels, which often ended with her father's entrance into the room she shared with her older sister. She would lie in her bed, stiff with hope and fear, but he always joined her sister and never came to her. Sometimes she could hear them "doing it," and she wished it were she sharing this experience. She had never talked about this with anyone before, but she knew her sister realized that their bad relationship had grown out of her jealousy. She then despairingly asked what was wrong with her that her father never once had approached her.

For years she had succeeded in putting all that away and not thinking of it. She had never realized until the last session how she was repeating the whole scene in her own marriage. She hadn't said so then, but was aware, that she usually picked the fights and "they are so silly, it's as though I just have to go through a ritual."

She expressed anger toward her mother who had never interefered—had never acted like a mother. She had not noticed that she, herself, had not acted like a mother until last week. She expressed surprise that she was feeling more relief than embarrassment now that she had told this story.

These two sessions were the crucial ones in a continued therapy. When the social worker modeled firm, protective mothering behavior, she not only provided an explicit lesson in parenting, but also implicitly signaled her acceptance of Mrs. T.'s need for a limit-setting, nurturing relationship within which she could safely unburden herself of painful, suppressed material that was forcing her into compulsive, repetitive, destructive behavior. Again, the focus was Mrs. T.'s current inner conflict and that between her and the most significant other people in her life. As with Mrs. O., the therapist cooperated with the client, who had the lead in determining the direction and the rapidity of the therapy, the stated goal of which in both cases was to examine the marital relationship.

THE FAMILY SYSTEM

Social work was the first of the helping professions to concern itself with the treatment of relationships between spouses and between parents and children. The early charity organization societies altered their function over time; as government took over the task of providing financial assistance to those in need they began to focus on family counseling as a primary function. In the child guidance clinics, social workers treated the parents of the children and worked to improve the family interaction patterns as well as the personality difficulties of the individual members. By 1940 Gordon Hamilton was describing the difficulties of "family group" treatment. Robert Gomberg's "The Specific Nature of Family Casework" was published in 1944. This was the first formal statement about marital and parental roles as the focus for family counseling (Perlman, 1974). This same social worker introduced Nathan Ackerman to the Jewish Family Service in New York City where the social work staff was spearheading the Family Therapy Movement. Hollis' *Women in Marital Conflict* appeared in 1949. This is a pioneering research endeavor in which the case records of a family service agency were studied to ascertain the psychological bases of marital conflict and the components of succcessful treatment. Hollis concluded that psychotherapy, based on a careful diagnostic understanding, was indicated.

THE STRESS OF DEPRIVATION

Today social work therapists are involved with people of all socioeconomic classes who are seen in a multitude of health and human service organizations, including industrial plants and the therapists' private offices. But their roots were in the homes of the poorer and otherwise disadvantaged. Even today, social work serves this group and is committed to it. Probably no other profession has produced more information about the psychological and social effects of and responses to noxious societal stressors such as chronic poverty, emotional deprivation, child abuse, parental loss, social isolation, chronic and acute illness, mental and physical handicaps, and on and on. Social work has attempted interventive strategies with the "multiproblem" families, the crisis-prone individuals, "the hard to reach," the hostile-dependent, and otherwise troubled people. The profession has devised and advocated large-scale public policies and practices for prevention and correction and denounced those which perpetuate misery; on a case-by-case basis social workers have been trying to assuage the misery as well as to advocate for the individual involved.

One of the most eloquent books written for the helping professions is Towle's (1945) *Common Human Needs*. It aimed to clarify the fact that public assistance in itself provides no basic psychological principles or psychotherapeutic ways to approach human beings; and it is as pertinent today as in 1945. This small volume addresses the importance of meeting individual need through direct personal methods while at the same time altering national economic policy. Anyone who wants to learn how to help people to improve their lot in life could start with this book, which explains individual psychodynamics and family interaction patterns as well as a variety of responses to stress.

THE DYNAMIC OF TIME

Social work has also contributed to the understanding of the process of psychotherapy. The Pennsylvania School of Social Work, in the 1930's under the leadership of Jessie Taft, formulated the "functional approach" to social casework. Although this approach engendered much controversy, many of its ideas have been incorporated into the mainstream of social work practice. One of its principles has found its way into general psychotherapeutic practice as well. A paraphrase of this is that the effectiveness of any psychotherapeutic process is furthered by the therapist's conscious use of time phases (beginnings, middles, and endings) in the process so that the potential of each time phase for the client may be fully utilized (Smalley, 1970). Responsibility is placed on the therapist to recognize and to respond to the differing needs of the client at different points in the treatment relationship. It suggests that therapy should have a finite duration, which should be set at the beginning of the process. This was a revolutionary departure from that traditional psychotherapy, which had no set time frame and often continued indefinitely, especially when the goals were fuzzy.

Today, unfortunately, time limits are often used for administrative rather than therapeutic reasons. However, brief or time-limited psychotherapy has been developed within all the disciplines. In addition, the principles of time and goal, when appropriately and judiciously used, have proved to be therapeutically useful.

SUPERVISION

Possibly the most pervasive and direct influence of social work upon the psychotherapeutic activities of all professions has been in the area of education and training. Social work education began in the early 1900's during the period of the charity organizations and prior to the professionalization of social work. As benevolence gave way to scientific effort, there were many who had gained some knowledge and skill through their experience in collecting data and in helping people. They began to teach novices on a one-to-one basis. As these instructors were, in addition, delegated administrative responsibility, they were given the title "Supervisor." Because of the material that is studied, part of which consists of awareness by the practitioner of his or her own values, attitudes, behaviors, and psychodynamics, this individualistic tutorial method has continued for both the student and the beginning professional social work clinician. When social workers began to be employed in hospitals in 1905, this method of educating students and new staff went with them, and was observed by their psychiatric colleagues who adopted the process for training psychotherapists.

There is extensive social work literature on supervision as an educational process. Towle's (1954) *The Learner in Education for the Professions* is useful to other professions. There is recognition of the similarities in the nature of the emotional response to learning psychological content, regardless of discipline.

SUMMARY

Other social work literature has been of consistent use to many varied professional groups. Most outstanding of these is Garrett's (1942) *Interviewing, Its Principles and Methods,* which has remained in continuous use since its publication. Social work's contributions have been influential. Increasingly many are being better understood and adopted in the practice of psychotherapy. They can be listed as follows:

Person-in-situation. The social work orientation to clients as persons in dynamic interaction with their social-economic environment in all of its realities has helped to expand the understanding of all psychotherapists, although they have not necessarily altered their style of practice.

Environmental stress. Social work has contributed extensively to knowledge used by all the helping professions about the psychological and physical effects of and the psychological responses to noxious environmental stresses, such as chronic or sudden poverty, physical illness, mental illness, handicapping conditions, and geographic and cultural dislocation, as well as to knowledge about psychotherapeutic intervention with disadvantaged people.

Modification of the environment. That aspect of social work psychotherapy that most distinguishes it from all other disciplines is an emphasis upon modification of the client's social-economic environment, where necessary, and/or of helping the client to deal with it constructively.

Self-determination. Social work psychotherapy respects clients' right to determine their own growth goals and works with them within their own value systems and cultural patterns to realize them.

Nurturance. Social work psychotherapy recognizes that growth is fostered when unmet dependency needs are gratified.

Ego Support. Social work psychotherapy seeks primarily to strengthen clients' egos and to improve their self-images so that they can overcome their difficulties in living caused by either their own dysfunctional behavior and relationships or noxious social environments or both.

Reality and Transference. Social work psychotherapy not only uses the client's transference responses to the therapist, but augments this by understanding current object relationships and involves the client's ego in working out active solutions to problems with the goal of achieving growth. Clients are helped to obtain skills that will improve social functioning with others and to recognize and relinquish counterproductive transferences to family members, authority figures, peers, or other significant members within the immediate social environment.

Family and group. Social work psychotherapists were the progenitors of family and marital therapy as well as group therapy and have contributed significantly to the knowledge of family dynamics and interaction patterns.

Time and focus. Social work psychotherapists contributed new understanding of the meaning of time in psychotherapy and the value of its conscious use as a therapeutic tool to limit the length of an episode of treatment to increase its effectiveness. In addition, psychotherapists of other professions have incorporated into their practice the social work technique of focusing on current conflicts in the beginning stage of treatment.

Supervision. Clinical social work supervision is the model for psychotherapeutic training in all professions today.

This listing is not complete, but it does demonstrate the coherence and value of social work psychotherapy. The possibility of continued creative change exists. As social work psychotherapy responds to the changing human condition, it enriches not only the clients who use it, but the field of psychotherapy itself as well.

REFERENCES

Austin, L. M. Qualifications of Social Caseworkers for Psychotherapy. *American Journal of Orthopsychiatry*, 1956, 26, 47–57.

Bandler, L. Some Casework Aspects of Ego Growth Through Sublimation. In J. J. Parad and R.R. Miller (Ed) *Ego-Oriented Casework: Problems and Perspectives*. New York, Family Service Association of America, 1961

Coleman, J.V. Distinguishing Between Psychotherapy and Casework. *Social Casework*, 1949, 30, 244–251.

Committee on Psychiatry and the Community, *The Psychiatrist and Public*

Welfare Agencies. Group for the Advancement of Psychiatry, Report No. 94, 1975.

Garrett, A.M. *Interviewing, Its Principles and Methods.* New York, Family Welfare Association of America, 1942.

Group for the Advancement of Psychiatry. *On Psychotherapy and Casework.* Group for the Advancement of Psychiatry, Report No. 71, 1969.

Hamilton, G. *Theory and Practice of Social Casework.* New York, Columbia University Press, 1940.

Hamilton, G. Psychoanalytically Oriented Casework and Its Relationship to Psychotherapy. *American Journal of Orthopsychiatry.* 1949, 19, 209.

Hollis, F. *Women in Marital Conflict.* New York, Family Service Association of America, 1949.

Hollis, F. Contemporary Issues for Caseworkers. In J. J. Parad and R. R. Miller (Eds.) *Ego-Oriented Casework: Problems and Perspectives.* New York: Family Service Association of America, 1960.

Hollis, F. *Casework, A Psycho-Social Therapy.* New York: Random House, 1964.

McBroom, E. Socialization and Social Casework. In R. Roberts and R. H. Nee (Eds). *Theories of Social Casework.* Chicago: University of Chicago Press, 1970.

Perlman, H. H. The Problem Solving Model in Social Casework. In R. Roberts and R. H. Nee (Eds). *Theories of Social Casework.* Chicago: University of Chicago Press, 1970.

Perlman, H. H. *Confessions, Concerns and Commitment of an Ex-Clinical Social Worker.* Occasional Paper No. 5. Chicago: University of Chicago Press, 1974.

Richmond, M. *What Is Social Casework.* New York: Russell Sage Foundation, 1922.

Smalley, R. E. The Functional Approach to Social Casework. In R. Roberts and R. H. Nee (Eds.) *Theories of Social Casework.* Chicago: University of Chicago Press, 1970.

Towle, C. *Common Human Needs.* Washington, D.C.: Federal Security Agency, 1945. Reissued by National Association of Social Workers, 1957.

Towle, C. Casework Methods of Helping the Client to Make Maximum Use of His Capacities and Resources. Address to National Conference of Social Work, Atlantic City, N. J., April 1948.

Towle, C. *The Learner in Education for the Professions: As Seen in Education for Social Work.* Chicago: University of Chicago Press, 1954.

Beyond the Master's Degree: Education for Social Work Psychotherapy

ALTHOUGH ONE MIGHT wish that the master's degree program in social work would result in a highly skilled and proficient worker, this will never be the case because proficiency and excellence in any profession require discipline and slow maturation. Of social work education, Towle (1954) said:

It has become clear that, under educational systems highly favorable for the attainment of the profession's educational aims, the two short years afforded the learner may not make possible thorough grasp and integration of learnings so that he is able immediately to use them freely for their further intrenchment ...

There is a recognized need for the field of practice to share the responsibility of professional education through agency programs which afford students a period following completion of their master's degree work when they would be regarded as interns for whom there would be a planned progression of work with well-defined educational aims (pp. 409, 411).

Thus understanding is operationalized in the two registers of clinical social workers: the National Registry of Health Care Providers

---

This chapter is based on a paper presented to the National Board of Directors of the National Federation of Societies for Clinical Social Work meeting in Indianapolis, Ind., November 3, 1979. It was accepted as an official Federation policy.
*Members: Florence Lieberman, Betty Gray, Roberta Greene, Cheryl Gropper, Jill Iselhard, Bert L. Kaplan, Tom K. Kenemore, Jean Orr, Trudy Persky, Matilda Rubin.

in Clinical Social Work (1978) and the NASW Register (1978). Each requires a minimum of two years of post-master's practice in clinical social work under the supervision of a social worker who has a master's degree (the National Registry of Health Care Providers in Clinical Social Work specifies a "graduate clinical social worker").

Supervision, intensive case consultation, in-service training seminars, and staff development programs have been methods traditionally used for the continued development of clinical skills among agency employees. Agencies that provide the most intensive in-service clinical programs are commonly viewed as the most desirable employers. In addition, social workers who wish to refresh their knowledge enroll voluntarily in summer workshops offered by schools of social work. Professional meetings and workshops of varying degrees of intensity and sponsorship are other sources of professional development—social workers participate in great numbers in workshops and meetings sponsored by their own discipline and other disciplines, such as the American Psychiatric Association, the American Psychoanalytic Association, the American Orthopsychiatric Association, and the American Group Psychiatric Association.

But these learning opportunities do not provide what Towle describes as "the planned progression of work with well-defined educational aims." For example, in-service training seminars and staff development programs tend to vary in depth and range, to be dependent on the needs and resources of the agency, and to stress the services and skills required by the agency. Inadequate attention is paid to the individual clinician's learning needs.

Supervision and intensive case consultation are time-honored methods of teaching and learning in clinical fields. Ideally, the supervisory process relies on the individual case study as the medium for individualized instruction. Although didactic, this method is also experiential because it deals with personal reactions and understanding. Intensive case consultation—the in-depth study of one or a series of cases—may be furnished by a member of the social work profession or by a representative of another discipline. In either case, however, it should provide an opportunity for a study of long-term process and practice.

Social work practitioners across the United States are clamoring for advanced training. Many are attending training institutes under the aegis of other professions, which seldom accord adequate recognition of the identity and values of clinical social work and have only minimal representation of social workers as faculty. Although increasing numbers of schools of social work are developing integrated continuing education programs or university doctoral programs, only a few focus on a knowledge base that adequately meets the demands of clinical practice.

It is the existence of current problems and need within the field of clinical social work that prompted the National Federation of Societies for Clinical Social Work to present a proposal for post-master's education in clinical social work. The type of post-master's clinical education proposed here differs from the increasingly required but sporadic credits in continuing education: It is directed toward the development of practitioners for advanced-level functioning in clinical social work, that is, toward the development of social work psychotherapists.

DEFINITION

Pinkus et al (1977) defined the clinical social worker as:

a health-care provider for individuals alone, in families and in groups where there are problems in biopsychosocial functioning. These problems may be the result of internalized personality dysfunctioning or created and maintained by social, health or economic stress or the consequence of the internalization of persistent external stress or the end result of a combination of personality factors and social, health and economic difficulties. The objectives of the clinical social worker are both preventive and remedial and the methods used are varied ... (p. 260).

The practice of advanced clinical social work is a developing and increasingly distinguishable form of psychotherapy. It contains all the structural elements of a form of psychotherapy, including treatment techniques, practice methodology, theories about change and the goals of change, and behavioral science theory. The objectives of psychotherapy—bringing about positive behavioral change and ego growth to improve individual functioning—are consistent with the objectives of clinical social work practice. In addition, advanced practice of clinical social work must reflect the integration of social work's mission and psychotherapeutic methodology.

The relatively consistent and stable thematic notion about purpose and mission that repeatedly emerges in the social work literature is derived from the profession's system of values. Stated simplistically, the notion is that the purpose or mission of social work practice is improvement of the relationship between individuals and their social environment. Regardless of the extent to which one distinguishes clinical social work from other social work activities, this notion must be included in the description and definition of clinical social work if it is to remain a part of the field.

When clinical social work is viewed from this perspective, it is possible to predict that if practice methodology is delineated, taught, and applied in terms that relate to social work (improvement of the relationship between individuals and their social environment), and if practice methodology is further developed within the scientific framework that characterizes psychotherapy, clinical social work practice will be solidly identified as a psychotherapeutic specialization within the broader field of social work practice.

GOALS OF CONTINUING EDUCATION

Before one can identify the steps needed to achieve the end product of a postgraduate training program, one must determine what the end product should be—just as one must establish treatment goals before proposing a treatment plan. Several questions arise during any attempt to describe a product: (1) In what terms does one most appropriately describe an expected, or hoped-for, product? (2) Who should describe the product? (3) How does one relate the described product to the steps proposed to achieve it? (4) How does one assess the utility and quality of the product once it is achieved?

Webster's definition of a product as "anything produced, as by generation, growth, labor, or thought" includes several definitions of "produce." The definition most fitting for our purpose is "to cause to be or to happen; to originate; to bring about." In human social terms the product we propose to offer is a fairly specific set of skills or, in Webster's terms, "a particular art or science; ... or a developed or acquired ability."

The specific set of abilities expected of graduates of postgraduate training programs are those that will enable technicians to provide the essential services with some degree of consistency. These abilities are many but can be listed under two broad categories. The first category can be called differential diagnosis and treatment, a conceptualization that underlies the description of the essential curriculum and training content of a postgraduate program. This category may include the following abilities:

1. To establish a differential biopsychosocial diagnostic assessment based on a specialized body of knowledge.
2. To establish a basic treatment plan derived from the psychosocial diagnostic assessment.
3. To establish progress through specific steps, leading to completion of the treatment plan.
4. To select from and carry out alternative treatment strategies (including variations in modality and duration).
5. To engage in continuous, objective, and systematic evaluation of treatment.
6. To practice independently.

Differential diagnosis and treatment of the person– problem–situation gestalt is a conceptualization that also suggests boundaries to advanced clinical social work training. Psychotherapy training that elaborates diagnosis and treatment of only *one* part of this configuration and neglects the others would be excluded from the framework. For example, a social worker can legitimately pursue training in psychoanalysis, family therapy, behavioral treatment, child psychotherapy, gestalt therapy, or political advocacy without necessarily having this training included in the definition of advanced clinical social work training. The principles and definitions mentioned earlier suggest that a postgraduate training program in clinical social work must elaborate, as its central purpose, training that will enable the clinical social worker to diagnose and treat persons differentially in relation to social problems as well as to intrapsychic problems while focusing attention on the interrelatedness of these problems.

The second broad categorization of skills can be called self-evaluation. This category relates to the need to maintain and increase the quality of one's skills and includes the following abilities.

1. To demonstrate an independent and high level of competence in carrying out one's practice skills.
2. To communicate one's rationale for a particular course of intervention to others, using commonly understood and utilized theoretical behavioral science and practice knowledge.
3. To make contributions to behavioral science and practice knowledge that are relevant to the field of clinical social work.

4. To utilize self-awareness in an integrative manner in relation to one's practice.

This may require selective use of consultation or personal psychotherapy. Personal therapy contributes to clinical excellence by enabling self-awareness and the ongoing process of self-evaluation, which is an integral part of responsible and accountable clinical work. The expansion of self-awareness, which includes an understanding of the unconscious motivation of behavior, ensures that clinical actions with clients will be determined by knowledge and self-knowledge and used to the client's therapeutic advantage (Blanck, 1973).

Thus all clinical social work practitioners should be encouraged to consider personal therapy as a method of enhancing self and practice. However, personal therapy *should not be* a part of the educational process. In addition, under *no* circumstances should a member of the program's faculty be the therapist for a candidate in the program.

AUSPICES

The responsibility to provide for advanced continuing education of clinical social workers belongs to both the academic and practice sectors of the profession. Ideally, a program that exists under the auspices of an accredited school or university is advantageous for reasons such as facilities, funding, recognition, formal and generally accepted credit structure, accountability, and review. Too often, however, there is a dichotomy between university-based faculty who do not practice and clinical practitioners who do not teach. In all other professions professional school faculties are expected to practice and to have outstanding clinical skills. Schools of social work and the universities with which they are affiliated often do not accord this recognition. This problem has been addressed by the Post-Master's Program in Clinical Social Work at the Hunter College School of Social Work (City University of New York), and Caroff (1977) has stated that collaboration of sophisticated clinical social workers and academicians who are also in clinical practice assures the relevance of content for teaching and learning. Caroff also points out, however, that universities and schools of social work must find ways to credit and reward clinical practitioners adequately for their participation. Some schools committed to clinical programs, at the master's as well as advanced level regularly use clinicians as educators, but in too many schools this does not occur. As a result, training institutes are developing under the control of a variety of social work organizations, including some state members of the National Federation of Societies of Clinical Social Work.

Advanced clinical training can be part of a doctoral program in social work. Although the program may need to include a series of courses that satisfy requirements for doctoral work, it must include some of the proposed guidelines to meet the specificity of clinical education. Many social workers are less interested in the higher degree than they are in obtaining advanced skill. For them, certification programs may be equally satisfactory.

Continuing education outside of university auspices also can have positive aspects. For example, when schools do not have master's programs that are clinically oriented or when these programs are anticlinical, it is paradoxical for them to attempt advanced education in clinical practice. Programs under a variety of other auspices or organizations may then provide a stimulus to schools of social work. There may be opportunities for creative educational practices and for experimentation with new ways of developing clinicians. Sometimes services agencies that have employees with specialized experience and knowledge or expertise concerning a particular area, population, or problem are geared to educate, teach, and enable continued and formalized clinical training. For all programs, regardless of auspices, some accountability and controls, both of the institution and of its students, are essential.

CORE CURRICULUM

The core curriculum of a program designed to prepare for advanced-level functioning in clinical social work psychotherapy revolves around many dimensions of knowledge related to individuals in their family and social environments. This includes a base for competent assessment and diagnosis and the skill for appropriate practice implementation related to individuals and environments. Thus knowledge and skill must be thorough and precise enough to permit incisive and systematic practice that is consistent with the needs of specific clients and must be broad, generic, and holistic enough to assure a direction of practice that views the client as part of a larger social system, encompassing more than the relationship and happenings within the therapeutic encounter. This dual focus is an inherent aspect of the curriculum.

Hartmann (1939) discussed this dual focus in his psychoanalytic development psychology (ego psychology) and his consideration of adaptation and fitting together. Beginning with an essential recognition of Freud's contributions to psychoanalytic theory, Hartmann elaborated on the intricate relationship between processes that are internal to the individual, the individual's manner of interacting with the environment, and the environment's influence on the individual. Knowledge of this interrelationship as well as of each distinct polarity (unconscious, individual process in interaction with larger social processes) is essential for competent practice. To reflect this orientation, the core curriculum of advanced-level practice should include developmental, diagnostic, interpersonal, organizational, and practice theory; accountability and evaluation; and values and professional ethics.

Developmental Theory

A basic understanding of the human condition includes knowledge about the individual at various stages of growth and development to provide perspectives concerning age-appropriate and phase-specific internal unconscious and external processes. This enables the practitioner to organize and interpret data in accordance with developmental direction. Whereas this knowledge began as a function of reflective philosophic inquiry into the nature of humans, recent investigations have provided more consistent and integrated information that is closely related to biopsychosocial and cognitive processes.

Theories of pathologic development emerge as a natural by-product of a developmental orientation that views the person as a growing organism passing through increasingly complex levels of functioning (stages) during his or her lifetime. If each level is viewed as having more or less expectable characteristics, deviations from those expectations can be observed and inferences can be made concerning their etiology.

Developmental theory necessarily includes knowledge of the individual as interacting with and as part of a larger social system. Because, to some extent, polarities have been established between individualistic and sociological processes, distinct and separate bodies of knowledge exist and a common vocabulary has not yet been adequately developed. Thus, in addition to concepts relating to individual processes, other concepts are needed to study the family, couple, or group, including those that approach behavior from a social interactive perspective and emphasize the impact of the social situation on the human condition. In other words, the social work psychotherapist is expected to be familiar with developmental processes from the biological, psychological (ego-oriented and object-related), cognitive, and social-interactive perspectives.

Diagnostic Theory

In keeping with the knowledge base, diagnostic formulations should be related to developmental processes, taking into account the various developmental milestones, strengths, and deficits that have occurred as well as the complexities of development that may have caused deviations from age-expectable and phase-specific constellations. These formulations offer a diagnostic organization that implies therapeutic direction and an approach consistent with social work orientation, values, ethics, and philosophy.

At the same time, diagnostic thinking has been characterized by a medical model in which clusters of symptoms are the basic organizing concepts. This has resulted in the use of classificatory schema that basically are unrelated to therapeutic prescription or developmental processes. Because the medical model is still commonly used among the mental health professions, one must be familiar with these symptom clusters, as categorized in the DSM-III.

Interpersonal Theory

In contrast with developmental theory, in which interactional behaviors are viewed as a function of intrapsychic processes, the focus of interpersonal theory is on interactional processes and sequences. Although interpersonal theory has led to some conceptual distinctions in relation to couples, families, and groups, its proponents have yet to formulate a relatively consistent, coherent, and generally acccepted theory base. Instead, there are many theories; all have their proponents and all are in the process of development.

Organizational Theory

Social work is traditionally practiced within some type of institutional setting. Although many social workers are engaged in private practice, this is often a part-time commitment, frequently occurring as part of a group practice that has its own organizational components. Therefore, it seems only natural to expect the social work psychotherapist to be sophisticated about the impact of organizational functioning and processes on type, quality, and offering of practice. This sophistication enables a better understanding of how the setting influences the worker and the client, and their interactions. It also facilitates helping a client negotiate a particular system when such an action is diagnostically indicated.

Practice Theory

Theories of human development, need, and deviance; theories of systems and the like; and theories of practice are interdependent and inseparable. Yet theories that enhance understanding are not identical to theories of practice or "doing." Many complex and intricate processes are involved in operationalizing conceptual formulations and in implementing therapeutic direction. A practice theory that focuses solely on methods and components of practice without paying attention to theoretical explanations of effectiveness is insufficient.

Practice must be derived from theoretical underpinnings; technique must flow from theory rather than from a practice preference. Services must be consistent with an understanding of clients' needs in relation to their environments. Thus it is possible to use a variety of methods. For in-depth skill, however, the social work psychotherapist must be extremely competent in the use of relationship skills required in individual treatment. Other methods—group, family, marital—may be specialized practice skills that build on the theoretical knowledge base that is the underpinning of advanced study.

Accountability and Evaluation

The process of accountability is regarded as synonymous with administrative responsibility between agent or agency, and it is supported by clients, a citizens' board, or funding agents. Included in accountability are assessment, operational plans, and acceptability and utilization of services.

Evaluation is a process of determining value or degree of success in achieving program or treatment goals using such criteria as cost, efficiency, and effectiveness of outcome. To assess properly what works with whom and how effectively, it is necessary to use the orderly procedures of science to evaluate the techniques of inducing change on the basis of established criteria. These procedures should cover areas subsumed under accountability and evaluation.

The knowledge gained through this type of assessment is important because it helps the advanced practitioner to evaluate professional and clinical research and literature, encourage contributions to this research and literature, and engage in activities related to the growth of professional standards review operations and to general program evaluation and planning. The challenge is to achieve more specificity in determining how traditional or innovative therapies can be applied to specific treatment problems and to develop ways of assessing whether treatment modalities under study are actually carried out as intended.

Values and Professional Ethics

Ethics prescribe obligatory actions (Levy, 1976). A variety of social work values conform to ethical obligations related to social enhancement of clients through meeting of needs and protecting the rights of individuals. Clarification of social work values and the ethics underlying practice is an essential aspect of an advanced curriculum. This affirms and heightens identification with the profession of social work and acts as a guiding principle for professional behavior.

CLINICAL CURRICULUM

Although classes and books help one to learn about clinical processes, only with practice over time can one become a clinician (Kubie, 1971). The professional "does"; it is in the doing that the various components of professional action, the theory that informs, the knowledge that enhances, and the values and techniques that direct are integrated and synthesized into a utilitarian whole.

A clinical component should consist of three parts: clinical practice, supervision, and a practicum. It is important for students to be engaged in a current practice that provides a base for application and study of the various components of an advanced clinical program. This practice can take place in a variety of settings and be conducted under the supervision of an advanced clinical social worker (one who meets the qualifications of a social work psychotherapist).

Supervision is concerned with intensive in-depth study of case material selected from the candidate's current practice. The emphasis should be on the process of therapy, and theory should be integrated into practice.

The practicum offers another opportunity to integrate practice theory, personality theory, and other aspects of core knowledge. And if it involves several candidates in a group experience, it provides an opportunity for in-depth study with other professionals for examination of material other than one's own. The practicum should enable a dynamic and scholarly process of applying theory to practice and permit discussion of differences and similarities in approach and technique. It also demonstrates the value of openness and sharing among professional peers and suggests another model for autonomous practice. Although the group should be led by an experienced social work psychotherapist, the supervisory process includes the group members as well as the leader.

EVALUATION OF OUTCOME

Evaluation of outcome should precede credentialing of candidates. In addition to successful completion of course requirements, candidates should supply additional evidence of competence, optimally by presenting a sample of their own practice to a qualified panel. Competence would be based on evidence of an integration of values and knowledge and a level of skill deemed necessary for self-directed, independent practice (Caroff, 1977).

SPECIALIZATION

Although social work psychotherapy can be viewed as a specialty within social work, specialization within social work psychotherapy comes *after* one achieves competence in psychotherapy with individuals and should be regarded as an additional course of study. This additional course of study could involve learning to work with special populations such as children, adolescents, or the elderly, or learning to apply certain theory and techniques when working with entities such as groups, couples, or families. Treatment approaches such as crisis therapy and short- and long-term treatment are not specialties; they are essential aspects of practice knowledge for social work psychotherapy.

SUMMARY

The preceding program for advanced clinical social work practice is viewed as essential for development of social work psychotherapists. It is an ambitious program that requires commitment on the part of the candidates as well as the organizations involved in the educational process. If the basic objectives are kept in mind, this program should contribute to the development of the social work profession, and enhance the independence and creativity of the social work professional who works alone, in group practice, or under agency auspices. It should also develop practitioners who will contribute to the professional literature and become teachers and supervisors of beginning social workers and leaders in the field of clinical social work.

REFERENCES

Blanck, R. Countertransference in the Treatment of the Borderline Patient. *Clinical Social Work Journal*, 1973, 1(2), 112.

Caroff, P. The Post-Master's Program for Clinical Social Work: Conception, Birth, and Early Development. *Clinical Social Work Journal*, 1977, 5(4), 328–335.

Kubie, L. Retreat from Patients. *Archives of General Psychiatry*, 1971, 24.

Levy, C. *Social Work Ethics*. New York: Human Sciences Press, 1976.

NASW Register of Clinical Social Workers. Washington, D. C.: National Association of Social Workers, 1978.

National Registry of Health Care Providers in Clinical Social Work. Lexington, Ky, 1978.

Pinkus, H. et al. Education for the Practice of Clinical Social Work at the Master's Level: A Position Paper. *Clinical Social Work Journal*, 1977, 5(4), 253–268.

Towle, C. *The Learner in Education for the Professions*. Chicago: University of Chicago Press, 1954.

SELMA FRAIBERG

4

Psychoanalysis and Social Work: A Reexamination of the Issues

IN OUR PROGRAM at the Child Development Project, University of Michigan, we have sought to bring psychoanalytic principles to clinical work with young families whose babies are in trouble and are, as families, suffering grave disintegrative problems. These are mainly families in poverty. The largest number of them suffer from psychosocial diseases which have been transmitted over several generations. Many of our families are headed by teenage girls who are the mothers of babies in trouble. Many of our two-parent families are in danger of dissolution at the time we first meet them. Their babies are showing the signs of grave developmental disorders. A large number of the babies have been referred to us for neglect or child abuse.

In social work language these are the "multi-problem families" and the "hard to reach families." In clinical jargon they are the "unmotivated patients" and are regarded as unsuitable patients for psychotherapy. Certainly they have rejected the offers of help available in their communities. And they do not seek help in mental health clinics.

Our staff is composed of two psychoanalysts (including myself), three clinical psychologists, two social workers, and a pediatric

Reprinted by permission from *Smith College Studies in Social Work*, March 1978, 47:2, 87–106.

consultant. All of us are part-time and together we represent the full-time equivalent of 3.5 staff members. We serve over 140 families a year. There are no fees for our services. Our program is supported by NIMH and The Grant Foundation. Our research commitment to NIMH is a study of treatment outcome. The first of our outcome studies is well advanced at the time of this writing. We have chosen the first 50 cases in our intensive treatment group, mainly cases in the "very severe" range judged on the basis of developmental pathology in the infant and psychopathology of the parents. We have developed assessment measures pre-post treatment for this group. The treatment results have surpassed our expectations. The largest number of babies and families in this group, judged clinically at most severe risk, have been brought to adequacy in functioning, judged by very strict criteria. In the coming year we will submit our data to independent judges to test agreement and expect to publish our results in a detailed analysis following this final step.

The methods which have brought these favorable outcomes for a group of severely disordered babies and their families unite psychoanalytic principles and therapeutic techniques with old and traditional social work practices and a strong theoretical base in developmental psychology. The methods are the subject of today's discussion.

In what follows I will not attempt a detailed exposition of methods—this is better done through extensive clinical reports and can be examined in our published case reports (Fraiberg, Adelson and Shapiro, 1975; Shapiro, Fraiberg, and Adelson, 1976; Adelson and Fraiberg, 1977). Rather, I will attempt to select certain principles of psychoanalytic theory and psychoanalytic treatment and illustrate their applications to a new field of mental health.

We should begin, you will agree, with "transference."

TRANSFERENCE

The concept "transference" in psychoanalysis had its origins in the unique circumstance in which a patient with neurotic conflicts agreed to spend 50 minutes a day, five times a week, on the couch of a psychoanalyst where, according to the rules of therapy, he would attempt to speak without censorship the thoughts that emerged into consciousness. The analyst, who spoke little, offered himself as a screen on which pictures and ideas and affects were projected, and the process of examination of the repressed past emerged from this circumstance. Transference meant literally the transference of the past into *this* present in which the analyst became the new object of old conflicts and the process of unravelling the past was facilitated.

If one is conducting a psychoanalysis there is still no better method for the undoing of the past than the classical method, and the transference as vehicle is also central to the healing process. However, it would be a mistake to say that transference as a phenomenon can *only* exist in the psychoanalytic situation.

Transference is the unconscious repetition of the past in the present, in which contemporary figures are endowed with the qualities of significant figures in the unremembered past. In this sense transference is not alone an occurrence which is elicited by the psychoanalytic situation (although the psychoanalytic situation is designed to enhance it). It is present in everyday life, and manifests itself most strongly under conditions of emotional conflict. Since we, as social workers, most frequently see patients who are in severe emotional conflict, we are bedeviled by old ghosts in the patient's past and whether we can reach the patient and find out where it hurts, may depend entirely upon the wisdom borrowed from psychoanalysis.

In what follows I will bring together a group of case illustrations. The thought occurs to me now that I might use two vocabularies, one a conventional vocabulary in social work and the other a psychoanalytic vocabulary, to describe what we see in these cases.

Gwen and Trudy

I will begin with the case of 16-year-old Gwen and her 5-month-old daughter, Trudy. Gwen is unmarried and supported by AFDC. Trudy, the baby, is referred to us for failure to thrive. Her physical survival is in danger and her psychological development is greatly imperilled, as we will see shortly. The hospital in its referral to us describes Trudy as "suffering from severe maternal and emotional deprivation." Gwen, her mother, is described as grossly neglectful, indifferent to her baby, and hostile toward the physicians and social workers who are trying to help her. In conventional social work language Gwen might be labeled as "a rejecting mother," "an uncooperative patient," and a "hard to reach patient."

Edna Adelson of our staff is assigned as therapist soon after the referral comes to us. There is no question that Gwen is "hard to reach." Four weeks of phone calls and letters lead to broken appointments and, in fact, Mrs. Adelson does not meet Gwen and her baby until one month after the referral. Is psychoanalytic theory of any use when the patient has never appeared? And is it any help or consolation to the therapist who is in anguish knowing the dangers for the baby? During this period in which Mrs. Adelson firmly and tirelessly makes her attempts to meet Trudy and Gwen, she is fortified by her own clinical knowledge. A girl who takes flight from every attempt to set up even an initial appointment is very likely a terrified girl, a girl who has already endowed the unseen therapist with fantasies of a dangerous woman. But can we speak of "transference" before the patient has even met the therapist? Why not?

Finally, Mrs. Adelson, Trudy, and Gwen meet. The meeting takes place in a doctor's office in the hospital. There is Gwen, the schoolgirl mother, angry, sullen, impudent, tough, slovenly, exactly as described.

Gwen meets Mrs. Adelson with a tirade. Everyone is blaming Gwen for not feeding her baby. Everyone is blaming her because the baby throws up all the time. She keeps coming to this damn clinic every week for checkups, and the doctors haven't found out yet why Trudy throws up all the time. Edna Adelson listens patiently to this torrent. Out of the corner of her eye she sees Trudy in a bundle of rags, a limp little bundle herself with pipestem arms and legs, a solemn face, staring eyes. We should not ask Mrs. Adelson what is going on in her mind. If the impulse to pick up the baby and take her home has entered her mind, we would all forgive her (i.e., for the impulse). If the doctors and nurses and social workers at the hospital are frightened for Trudy and angry with this sullen, contemptuous child–mother, we can forgive them too.

The torrent goes on, a recital of grievances against the hospital, the day-care center, the ADC. She, Gwen, has been telling the doctors, and telling the doctors, that the baby throws up and they won't do anything. "They won't listen to me. Nobody listens to me. Nobody understands." (Not true, Mrs. Adelson thinks to herself, knowing that the whole staff in that clinic had devoted itself to Gwen and Trudy for weeks, and that it is Gwen who doesn't listen.) But Mrs. Adelson is hearing a message in this litany of shrill complaints. *"Nobody listens to me. Nobody understands."* Finally, Mrs. Adelson finds a moment to speak, "Well, then, if you have been trying to get answers and you feel that nobody is listening to you, then you have a right to feel angry at everyone who is trying to help you. I am listening very hard. I want to understand everything you are saying. If I do not understand you, you will have the right to be angry at me too. And you can tell me that."

With these words, there is a change in the atmosphere. Gwen

looks incredulous. Her voice softens. The flood of complaints begins to dry up. She begins to look like the frightened child she is, and Mrs. Adelson, the witch–mother, undergoes a transformation (as I interpret this session) and becomes, very simply, Mrs. Adelson, a therapist who knows a great deal about parents and babies.

In technical language, we would say that Mrs. Adelson "handled the negative transference" and "cleared the path to a positive therapeutic alliance." In fact, this first session became the critical session for establishing a relationship with Gwen which led to excellent therapeutic work and guidance on behalf of Trudy, which brought the baby to nutritional and psychological adequacy in a few months! It was by no means the only period in treatment in which the negative transference renewed itself and was interpreted, but, very clearly, if the negative transference had not been dealt with in this first session, there would probably not have been any further sessions. The outcome for Trudy would have been placement in a foster home. (More terrible was the chance that Trudy might not be alive in a few weeks.) The outcome for Gwen would have been a tragedy beyond repair.

But it was not only "handling the negative transference" that was crucial in the first session. Mrs. Adelson had picked up a thread in this litany of complaints. The repetition of the phrases *"Nobody listens to me. Nobody understands."* True, this is a common enough complaint among patients, but there was something in this refrain that called for a selective therapeutic response. When Mrs. Adelson responded it was to those words, and she used these words selectively in her statement to Gwen. Nobody can know in a first session what these phrases mean on the most profound level. But, in a few weeks, when we knew Gwen and Trudy better, these words had special poignancy.

Gwen had been a war orphan, found abandoned at the age of two on the streets of an Asian city. She was starving when she was admitted to an orphanage. She was still in a state of severe nutritional inadequacy and in psychological danger when she was adopted by an American family at the age of two-and-a-half. She was a screaming, terrified child during the first year in her adopted family. And *nobody could understand her.* She spoke in a foreign language. Perhaps she had the words in her native tongue to say "I am afraid" or "Hold me tight" or "Don't go away; I will be lost again" but there was no one to understand her in this foreign land. Which is also to say, in child language in any tongue, *"Nobody listens to me!"*

The tirade at the hospital had echoes from the past. There was now another starving and neglected baby, Gwen's own child. This baby, too , was about to be taken from her mother if Gwen could not care for her. As we reconstruct it, the room at the hospital was crowded with ghosts. There were in a sense two starving babies, Gwen and Trudy. The past and present merged as panic arose in Gwen. She was again a screaming child "lost and abandoned" and once again, "Nobody listens to me. Nobody understands me." Mrs. Adelson heard the words and responded explicitly to these words. In this way the therapeutic alliance began.

However we do it, it is always the same. The therapeutic relationship begins with "need" and "a responder to need."

As I write this clinical story I am suddenly caught short by the way in which the issues expanded. I had started by examining the issue of transference with a patient called "hard to reach." Within three pages of exposition, at least four other psychoanalytic ideas have appeared. The negative transference is addressed by the therapist and leads to "a positive therapeutic alliance." The range of the schoolgirl mother is seen as "a defense against anxiety." The mother who is starving her baby and in danger of losing her baby to strangers is seen as a girl who is "repeating the repressed memories of the past in the present." And the therapist, faced with a hostile neglectful teenage mother and a starving baby, can move emphatically in this taxing circumstance because she will not allow her own feelings to intrude, which is to say, she "handles her countertransference reactions."

In all these ways, then, psychoanalysis has guided the therapist in these most taxing circumstances, and the "hard to reach" patient has been "reached."

I am glad to report that this work with a "hard to reach" and "rejecting mother" has brought about most favorable changes in the baby and the mother. Within only a few weeks of work, the baby reached and sustained nutritional adequacy, and within the months that followed we saw a strong positive attachment develop between baby and mother.

Geri and Niki

Let's consider another patient, 17-year-old Geri and her 2-year-old daughter. Geri is black, unmarried, living with her mother and grandmother with AFDC support. Niki at 2 years of age is called "stubborn" and "mean" and "a faker," and "she won't mind anyone." Niki, seen in our office, is a sobering baby. She appears to have no attachment to her mother or to any other person. Mother and baby are in continual conflict and scream at each other "like two children" I was about to say, but that is exactly the case.

Geri did not see herself as a patient when she came to us. She seemed to be saying that we should change Niki since we were the baby specialists. She was uncertainly a mother and turned over a large part of Niki's care to her own grandmother and her mother, both of whom gave grudging care to the baby.

In several months of work with her first therapist in our program, who was a graduate student in social work training, Geri was a mainly silent patient. Whole sessions passed in painful silence, punctuated by rare exchanges when the therapist asked a question. And when Geri spoke her voice was flat, her face immobile. No anger, no sadness was registered.

In conventional language, Geri, then, was "hard to reach." She was also "nonverbal." And she was "unmotivated," not a promising candidate for therapy, if we read our texts. Following the therapist's completion of her training, Geri and Niki were transferred to one of our senior social workers, Vivian Shapiro. Mrs. Shapiro found the first sessions with Geri to be painful repetitions of all the sessions that had preceded. Silence. No visible affect.

Out of her own experience, Vivian Shapiro began to ask herself a number of questions. Is Geri "non-verbal" (meaning without a capability for using words) or is silence a form of transference resistance? Is the non-registration of affect an absence of affect or a defense against affect? These are useful questions which emerge from a psychoanalytic inquiry.

The silence of a patient occurs in psychoanalysis, too. Since most patients in psychoanalysis have established their credentials as persons with verbal capability, it is assumed that silence is a form of resistance or defense against painful affect. And "resistance," if we understand Freud well, is not obstinacy or uncooperativeness, but the summoning of a defense to ward off painful affect. The problem for therapist and patient is to examine the defense and allow the painful affects to emerge in the safety of the therapist–patient relationship.

There is no reason to believe that the ego and the mechanisms of defense are constituted in one way for the patient who pays $50 an hour and another way for the patient who pays no fee. There is no evidence, either, that the patient who holds academic credentials on a university level has been endowed with a richer affective life, a larger sensibility, a better capacity for introspection, or a more subtle vocabulary than the patient who is a high school dropout. I mean, well, you can have—like—a Ph. D. if you know what I mean, and sometimes you can't find the right words, if you know what I mean. Do you know what I mean?

As Geri's and Niki's therapist, Vivian Shapiro began to work with the highly plausible hypothesis that Geri's silence was a defense against painful affect, and that the defense was operating in the form of transference resistance. How to help Geri acknowledge and speak of her feelings toward the therapist? Mrs. Shapiro began with a cautious inquiry. Following one long episode of painful silence, the therapist said, very gently, "Geri, I think you must be very disappointed in me. You came to me for help and I am not helping you, am I?" Tears came into Geri's eyes and she nodded silently. Mrs. Shapiro then spoke to the tears and said that she wanted to understand Geri's feelings and very importantly, those feelings of disappointment in the therapist.

And, in the sessions that followed, Mrs. Shapiro returned to the theme "disappointment" in the therapist and suggested other feelings. She would not be surprised, she said, if Geri felt that she could not trust Mrs. Shapiro. After all, why should she? And slowly, hesitantly, Geri began to speak with eyes brimming over. Distrust, disappointment, and hurt led Geri to speak of herself, her mother, her grandmother. She remembered her pregnancy with Niki. She couldn't tell her mother for a long time. And when her mother learned that Geri was pregnant, she would not talk to her "for a long time." A cold, hostile silence was a family mode to express contempt. There was much more. Gery had always been the bad child in her family. And the worst thing she had done was to get pregnant at 15. Since Geri's mother herself had become pregnant out of wedlock, the word "bad" seemed unjust and somehow confounded by many family mysteries. Geri could not trust her mother or her grandmother. She kept her secrets to herself. And now, not surprisingly to an observing therapist, Geri was able to speak of a new secret; she was pregnant again. She was afraid that the therapist would think she was bad. She cried with relief when the secret was out.

All this took place in only a few sessions. The pathways in treatment followed this pattern: transference resistance and a therapeutic approach through the transference, "disappointment," "can't trust," the liberation of feelings of sadness. The pathways led to mother and grandmother, the first "helping persons" in Geri's life. When those first "helping persons" fail a child, who later become a patient, the transference to therapist in the initial phases is already distorted. The patient enters treatment with a built-in expectation that he will once again be disappointed, betrayed. He cannot speak because he cannot trust the therapist. Unless the therapist can deal with these feelings, there will be no help for the patient.

Once the pathways of feeling were opened up for Geri, she found words and she began the arduous therapeutic task of understanding and undoing her troubled past. And, since Niki was our patient, as well as her mother, it is good to report that the most remarkable changes took place in the relationship between Geri and her daughter. As Geri discovered the extraordinary experience of "being understood," "being heard," sharing her feelings with someone who could help, she became another kind of mother to Niki. She wanted to understand Niki. With Mrs. Shapiro she looked for reasons in Niki's behavior. And as Geri experienced psychological nurturance from her therapist, she became a mother who could tenderly nurture her own child. By the time the second baby arrived, Niki was making excellent progress in her own psychological development, Geri had found pleasure in being a mother, and the new baby was welcomed and cherished.

Throughout the last period of Geri's pregnancy, Carolyn Aradine, our nurse practitioner, joined Vivian Shapiro as a member of the therapeutic team. Miss Aradine brought psychological wisdom to her work with the very young mother who had once been the bad girl. As nurse, she ministered to the physical needs of a pregnant young woman. It was another form of caring that Geri had never known. And Geri understood that the baby within her, the "sinful" child in the eyes of Geri's mother and grandmother, was precious to Carolyn Aradine and Vivian Shapiro, because all babies are precious and one can't help the fact now that Geri is not married. But the painful realities of bringing a child into the world without marriage were also dealt with, honestly and fairly, in the therapeutic hours.

When Geri went into labor, she called Carolyn Aradine as planned. (Geri's mother refused to be with her.) And while Miss Aradine assisted in a normal and easy delivery, the baby was born, and within a few minutes Katy was placed in her mother's arms for a close embrace and Geri was radiant.

Geri, Niki, and Katy are a close family now. Geri is proud of herself and her children. She has taken a giant step toward psychological independence and a sense of self-worth. She has continued, after termination of treatment, to keep in touch with Vivian Shapiro and Carolyn Aradine to ask for guidance when problems occur (none serious) and to share good news. She has also learned to use birth control, which, not surprisingly, is something that one can do when babies are precious.

DEFENSE AND SYMPTOM FORMATION

In the second part of this paper I would like to examine the applications of psychoanalytic theory to the treatment of certain cases which have long taxed the resources of our social agencies and our courts; the multiproblem family in which social disease has been transmitted like a curse from one generation to another is one of these, and the youthful drug addict, growing in numbers and defeating the best efforts of our clinics, is another group.

Annie, Earl, and Greg

To illustrate the first group of cases I will choose a young family in our community which now represents the third generation pursuing an odyssey through courts, clinics, and placement agencies. By the time we meet the youngest generation, Annie is a 16-year-old girl, married to Earl, a 19-year-old boy, and they have a 4-month-old baby who is reported as neglected and in danger of abuse. The cycle has renewed itself.

Annie avoids her baby. The baby, tragically, avoids his mother with something that I read as fear in his eyes. Earl, the young husband, makes awkward attempts to give something to his son, to feed him when he has been left unfed, to hold him when he cries. But he, too, has given up under the pressure of overwhelming circumstances. And they are living in great poverty.

Annie has been labeled "a rejecting mother" and objectively this is so. But the label is not a diagnosis. It is a mailing address. Once the social agencies have placed the label on the mother, the destination is virtually certain. The family is routed to a network of social agencies, sometimes to four or five at once. If the rejecting mother does not become an unrejecting mother, the next address will be the court. After the court there may be a new address for the baby and a new address for the mother.

In this way, three generations of Annie's family, well known in our community, had been stamped and delivered to various ports in our community network. And the women in this family have continued to neglect their children, to abandon their children, to brutalize their children, and to form transient liaisons with alcoholic and abusive men.

Annie, herself, can speak of her childhood in a harsh, tough, street child voice. She can speak of brutal beatings by her stepfather. She can speak of the times when her mother abandoned her and her family and left them to fend for themselves. There is no anger and no pain in her voice.

It would be easy to add another label to Annie, "psychopathic personality" perhaps, or "borderline" personality. But these, too, can be mailing addresses. They do not tell us why a young girl who has suffered brutality and abandonment in her own childhood should repeat her past in the present.

In our work with Annie, Earl, and Greg, and many other young families, we have found it illuminating and ultimately most promising for change in personality and in the family to see this form of intergenerational transmission of social and personal psychopathology in psychoanalytic terms, as a form of defense, "identification with the aggressor." It is profitable for us to remember, too, that this form of defense is not peculiar to any particular family or personality. Very simply, we can see that when a person (child or adult) is the subject of tyranny, when the ego is brutally assaulted and pushed to the limits of tolerance or near extinction, the ego falls back upon an archaic defense, and allies itself with the enemy. In this way, many normal people who are the subjects of tyranny, as hostages, or political prisoners, can emerge from their experience with a strange and inexplicable bond with their jailers. In the case of a child reared by brutalizing parents, the young and immature ego cannot cope with the overwhelming anxiety induced by tyranny, and he defends himself against anxiety and disintegration of the ego by a form of psychological fusion with his attackers. He becomes like them and he doesn't know how this has happened because the process in identification is unconscious. From a dynamic point of view, identification with the aggressor protects the ego against overwhelming anxiety; as long as the defense is maintained, the ego can maintain anxiety in repression. When Annie tells her terrible story to the therapist, she does not remember the rage that must have been experienced at the times of assault and abandonment.

The treatment of Annie, Earl, and Greg is described in another paper (Fraiberg, Adelson, and Shapiro, 1975). The therapy took place entirely in the home. I will only touch upon one aspect of the work. The first and crucial part of the work during the beginning of treatment was to understand why Annie was avoiding her baby. The baby was in great danger. In the course of the early sessions we saw that avoidance for Annie was defense against her own destructive feelings. These feelings broke through at times in barely disguised messages to the baby and to the therapist. She was afraid that she would assault him, afraid that she might kill him. And we were afraid for the baby, too.

The most imperative therapeutic task was to protect the baby from the repetition of the mother's past. This meant, in psychoanalytic terms, that Annie needed to recover painful memories in the safety of the therapeutic relationship in order that the dangerous urges should be brought under control. This is a difficult therapeutic task under the most favorable circumstances, which is to say, in an analytic office with five treatment sessions a week. In this once or twice a week psychotherapy in a family living room or kitchen the task seemed formidable.

Why not another method? Why not provide supportive and educational guidance to Annie and persuade her to hold her baby, give him affection, and teach her to read her baby's signs? For some mothers this may indeed be a profitable form of treatment. But for Annie, we already knew this would not work. To be in close physical contact with her baby aroused the most frightening thoughts and impulses, as we saw in all of those early visits. The only alternative, as we saw it, was to deal with the frightening impulses in their place of origin, the tyranny of Annie's past. But might that not be dangerous too? If we spoke to the painful memories, brought them to consciousness with their attendant affects, might not the liberated affect lead to acting out against the baby himself? We considered this, too, and with trepidation. But if there are important lessons to be learned from psychoanalytic theory and experience, one of them is this: the danger of acting out is greater when affects are maintained in repression. They do their mischief in the dark. Our clinical hypothesis was that if Annie could remember her anxiety and helplessness before the attackers and abandoners of her past, the motive for her pathological identification with the aggressors could be modified.

And this became the guiding principle in the early weeks and months of treatment. As Annie was led with gentleness and sympathy to speak of her childhood horrors, Mrs. Shapiro chose the pathways to anxiety with delicate balance. As Annie spoke of her stepfather's brutality in her flat, cynical voice, Mrs. Shapiro spoke to a child's terror. "How frightening for a child," she said, and with open and heartfelt sympathy for that child. "There was no one to protect you. What can a child do?" It may have been the only experience in Annie's life in which someone understood and spoke to her helplessness and terror. It was, for Annie, a permission to feel. There were hours in which Mrs. Shapiro saw Annie's tough, street girl self dissolve before her eyes. The voice became small, the obese 16-year-old girl became small, if one can imagine it, and simple childhood terror and grief broke through with an eloquence that the street girl did not know she owned. At the close of one such hour Annie said, "I never want a child of mine to live through anything like that!" And her voice was fervent.

This marked the beginnings of great changes in Annie as Annie, and Annie as mother and wife. Annie began to move toward her baby, to respond to his need for her, to feel protective toward him, and to find pleasure and pride in him. And the domestic warfare between Annie and Earl began to subside.

Treatment continued for two years. I will not attempt to give details of the treatment which are described in another publication. For purposes of this presentation I will only say that for Annie, for Earl, and for Greg, the outcome of treatment has been a most happy one. Greg, who is now close to 5 years of age, is seen in a follow-up as a healthy, buoyant little boy, affectionate and endearing, confident in his mother's love for him and in her protection. A new baby brother, now 2 years old, testifies to the good mothering he is receiving and the good climate of his home. The marriage of Annie and Earl has become stable and it is the only stable marriage in their extended families. Annie, herself, is a proud and competent young woman. Last year, Annie, the high school dropout, enrolled in a class in child development. She was surprised, she told Mrs. Shapiro, to discover how much she knew.

The extended family is still in transit in our community. Grandmother, a deteriorating alcoholic, moves about from clinic to clinic. Annie's younger sister is psychotic and has been hospitalized. Still another sister abandons and reclaims her child at intervals, as harried social agencies label and relabel the disease which can't find a name. Annie, the survivor, now 21 years old, is a figure of awe and authority to her family. She is consulted by all members of her family, including her mother, as family crises occur. She dispenses wise counsel and keeps her own head. She thinks her mother and sisters all need therapy and has done her earnest best to persuade them, but not yet with success.

Ellen and Cindy

The second case which I will briefly describe is that of Ellen, a 22-year-old unmarried mother and her 18-month-old daughter, Cindy. Ellen, when we first met her, was a heroin addict and had been in and out of hospitals since she was 16. At 18, Ellen was diagnosed as schizophrenic and was hospitalized for many months. The diagnosis we now know was wrong.

Cindy was conceived in a mental hospital. By the time we met Cindy, she was a mute, terrified child, who clung to her mother as if she were a raft in a sea that was engulfing both of them. Cindy was being cared for in a daycare center. The center was alarmed by the deteriorating psychological state of both mother and child. Often, Ellen forgot to pick up Cindy at the close of the day. Many times Ellen was stoned when she arrived and carried the baby home in a trance. There was grave question for us and for the daycare people as to whether Ellen could use our help and whether placement of Cindy might not be the treatment of choice. But Ellen did not want to give up her baby. And in our county psychological neglect and psychological abuse of a baby do not constitute grounds for legal action.

Our own anxiety for both Cindy and Ellen was very great at the point we first met them, and for many months afterward. We began with the offer of an extended assessment and without a commitment to offer treatment. In our view, if we could not get help quickly to Ellen, on behalf of the baby, we would have to take some action to protect the baby, perhaps to bring Ellen to a voluntary plan for placement.

As the story of Ellen and Cindy unfolded in these first weeks, our own alarm increased. Ellen was caught up in a world of junkies and street people. She was supporting herself and her baby through AFDC, and some part of her meager AFDC allotment was supporting her drug habit. To maintain herself on drugs, she was borrowing heavily from friends and it was possible that another source of funds came from illegal transactions of one kind or another. She maintained contact with Cindy's father, Mike, whom she had met in a state hospital. He was a paranoid schizophrenic who was actively delusional and tyrannized Ellen when destructive rages broke through. Mike, and a ghostly procession of empty, solitary boys and men, all members of the drug community, were transient guests in Ellen's house and in her bed. Cindy was witness to scenes of violence in her mother's bedroom and was terrified of men. Sometimes she would waken in a household where everyone, including her mother, was stoned and she would pathetically try to rouse her mother.

In the face of all this madness, it is almost ludicrous to say that there were actually small signs of hope. Ellen, in intervals between heavy drug usage, was a mother who cared deeply for her baby. The thought of losing Cindy was terrifying to her. Vivian Shapiro was entirely honest with Ellen. If Ellen could not be helped to give Cindy the care and protection she needed, both Ellen and Mrs. Shapiro would need to think of placement in a foster home.

And Ellen, herself, in lucid moments, gave glimpses of hidden strengths in her personality. Thus, in spite of her fears that she might lose her baby, she allied herself with Mrs. Shapiro. Together they would try to make things better. And, as Ellen felt the strength and protection of her therapist, she began, very quickly it seemed to us, to give strength and protection to her baby. Ellen's own enormous need for a mother and for psychological nurturance became a psychological bridge to her child, helpless and in greater need than herself. We began to see, within the first months of treatment, as Ellen and Cindy met together in our office, that Ellen was using the relationship to Mrs. Shapiro and the guidance of Mrs. Shapiro in new and responsible ways for her child. Cindy was beginning to make developmental progress and Cindy we saw, with relief, was moving out of the frozen, terrified stance that had so alarmed us at the beginning. She was becoming a baby who was given the right to feel, to cry when necessary, to show anger when necessary and appropriate, and to ask for and receive attention.

But Ellen was still using drugs and, even though she was making valiant attempts to be a good mother to Cindy and to repair her damaged life, the risks of Cindy and for Ellen remained as long as Ellen was a drug user. Since Ellen had already been a patient in several community drug clinics and had abandoned each in turn, it seemed to us unprofitable to follow this route again. If Ellen could be helped, we were in the best position to help her. There was a strong positive relationship to Vivian Shapiro and our own clinic was well staffed to provide support for a difficult treatment.

Our own thinking began with certain questions and a clinical hypothesis which derived from psychoanalytic theory. The central question can be stated as follows: Why should a 22-year-old girl (or, for that matter, anyone else at any age) need a drug to produce euphoria or a brief ecstasy? Give the normal human capability for ecstasy through sexual experience, we can hypothesize that the drug user is incapable of erotic "highs" through normal sexual channels and is dependent upon the drug "high" as a substitute. Moreover, since the drug "high" is attained under conditions of self-abasement and through criminal transactions, our psychoanalytic inquiry leads us to consider that the drug use is also the acting out of repressed sexual fantasies in which self-abasement, self-inflicted pain, and the sense of being a criminal are all united in the substitute sexual experience. Theoretically, if we can find the links between drug usage and the original sexual conflicts, we can liberate the normal erotic capabilities of an Ellen and reverse the pathological process which had brought her to drug use.

What good is a theory? The theory led to the invention of methods in a twice-a-week therapy which brought about the liberation of Ellen from drug use and the liberation of her own sexuality. And it brought dramatic changes in personality.

I cannot do more than present a condensed account of Ellen's treatment in this brief exposition. As the therapeutic inquiry led into Ellen's sex life, we found what is almost certainly to be found in every drug user's experience. Ellen was incapable of erotic arousal under any circumstances which normally produce excitation and a culminating experience. Nor could she remember at the beginning of treatment any experience of genital arousal in childhood. What she could remember were exciting and morbid childhood fantasies in which dangerous and sadistic men attacked her. Slowly she began to see, with Vivian Shapiro's help, that for years she had been acting out these fantasies with men and drugs. But the drug "high" was all she had, she said, and she was manifestly fearful that Mrs. Shapiro might take away the only experience of ecstasy she knew. Mrs. Shapiro laid the groundwork for therapy carefully. If Ellen and she could work together to understand how sexual feelings had become distorted for Ellen and transformed into drug experience, Ellen would discover there was a greater pleasure in store for her, very simply, the erotic pleasures which resided in her own body. And on this basis the new work began, with Ellen's apprehensive consent.

Two visits a week were scheduled, but we must remember that we had two patients, Ellen and Cindy, and one session each week focused on Cindy with Cindy present. Ellen reserved the discussion of intimate material for her own private sessions and used the joint sessions with Cindy for observation of Cindy with Vivian Shapiro and for discussing day-to-day problems in child rearing. Understanding Cindy, however, was not alone a benefit to Cindy. As Ellen watched her own 2-year-old struggle with developmental problems she found another route into her own early childhood. Once, for example, Cindy was reprimanded by Ellen's mother for masturbating and Cindy's shame and hurt were painful for Ellen to witness. This led into two directions. First, how to help Cindy to understand that *her* mommy did not think touching genitals was a bad and shameful thing. Second, to help Ellen reflect that the mother who shamed Cindy might also have shamed Ellen and that Ellen's shame regarding her body and erotic feelings might have had their genesis in just such experiences.

In her private sessions, Ellen pursued the pathways which led back to her own childhood. Gradually, she could speak of the unspeakable, of erotic fantasies which involved her own father, and the recovery of erotic experiences with her father, shameful memories which brought back all the feelings of being crazy, sinful, worthless. Ellen found the links between the dangerous incestuous fantasies and her obsessive longing for dangerous men. She found the links between sadomasochistic fantasies and the invitation to abuse and beatings by men. As shame and self-abomination found words and reasons, Ellen became free of her past. And, as promised, Ellen discovered, that is, rediscovered sexual pleasure. She no longer needed drugs. Yet, there was one climatic experience, one last episode of acting out which completes the story. During one period when Ellen was facing the need to give up her erotic feelings toward her own father, she sought out Mike, Cindy's father. In their old style they were beginning the preparations for "shooting up" when suddenly Ellen was overcome with nausea. She vomited profusely and left without using the needle. From this point on, Ellen discovered that thoughts of drug use brought on a profound sensation of nausea. It was an extraordinary reversal and one that told us Ellen was on her way to cure. In short, the revulsion which had once attached itself to sexual feelings was now attached to drug use, which, we must conclude, is just where it should be.

Ellen is transformed in many ways. She is growing in self-confidence and has aspirations for herself which she had never known. She is attending college now, doing well, and moving steadily toward her own career goals. She has moved away from the street people and no longer needs them. She is a devoted mother to Cindy and has pride in her child.

Cindy, herself, is a delightful small girl who shows large strengths in her personality and in her ability to cope with the normal problems of her age. But we, who know her well, are aware of residues of her tragic infancy. Cindy is still fearful of men and we must help her with this problem And, still, today, long after Ellen has given up drugs, Cindy is watchful and anxious for her mother at ccertain times. If Ellen has the flu or a cold, Cindy will ask with urgency, "Mommy sick? Doan wanna go to Grandma's." We feel wounded for Cindy when we hear those words. Cindy will need all the help she can get from her mother and from us. Yet, we can reassure ourselves. What we have given Cindy, what her mother has given Cindy, is strength and adaptive capability during the period of ego formation. She has the possibility of finding adaptive solutions to life stresses. When we first knew her, she was immobilized by fear and regressing rapidly. Without help, in a critical period of development, Cindy could not have survived in the psychological sense.

REFLECTIONS

My "re-examination" of the place of psychoanalysis in social work brings me very close to my earlier examinations of these issues, which were first published about 25 years ago (Fraiberg, 1951, 1955, 1954). What has changed is only an enlargement of those views. As I, myself, grew more experienced and competent as a psychoanalyst and a social worker, the applications of psychoanalytic principles to social work embraced even more complex problems than those I had earlier envisioned.

If many of us here tonight are persuaded that psychoanalysis has brought an inexhaustible treasure to the practice of social work, we are also faced with the formidable problems of teaching the principles and the applications of psychoanalytic theory to students and young practitioners.

It is a difficult and demanding theory for the student. It cannot be mastered in the course of a few lecture sessions, or, regrettably, even in several years of study. But the student who acknowledges its complexities, its demands upon the intellect and personal emotional experience, has already taken a giant step. He has acknowledged the infinite complexity of personality and he may never again be satisfied with a psychology that offers easy answers and easy remedies for human ills. In the same moment that he takes this giant step, he takes another. For once he confers complexity and ambiguity to the constitution of personality in others, he must grant the same characteristics to himself, and can no longer exalt himself or dispense divine wisdom in the name of his profession.

This is the beginning of psychoanalytic wisdom. The rest can be gained through study, through the guidance of excellent teachers and supervisors, and the unparalleled instruction which the patient himself gives the therapist.

I was asked to touch briefly upon our curriculum and the methods of teaching psychoanalytic principles in our program at the Child Development Project. The heart of our training program for graduate students and staff resides in supervision. Every member of our staff, including the most expert clinician, consults regularly with a supervisor who can be me, or our consulting psychoanalyst, or another senior staff member. All supervision is based upon the process notes of the therapist. For the student we build in psychoanalytic theory through case discussion and through discussion of relevant readings, which are provided in our own good library. We augment this learning through our own intramural seminars, which are attended by staff and graduate students. We do not offer courses or a graded sequence of seminars in theory. For those who need to achieve grounding in psychoanalytic theory through course work, there are excellent courses available in our university. I am afraid that if an accrediting organization existed for the review of curriculum in the teaching of psychoanalytic principles to social workers, the Child Development Project might be thrown out. On the other hand, the graduates of our program can provide their own testimony that this teaching is highly effective. So, something can be said for our unconventional program, which has no graded course work, no formal curriculum, one which turns loose young and unripe students in the treacherous terrain of the library and the archaic pedagogy of the tutorial. What matters is that every member of our Project faculty is an excellent teacher; and if the curriculum on paper looks sparse, the curriculum in the supervisory and tutorial session is infinitely rich and demanding of the highest qualities in the student.

I believe that the future of psychoanalysis in social work resides with the teachers and not the curriculum. This audience offers its own testimony. This meeting of social workers in the Boston area is, in a sense, a celebration which honors great teachers who brought psychoanalytic principles to Boston social workers nearly 40 years ago. Helene and Felix Deutsch, Greta and Edward Bibring, Beata Rank, and their own distinguished students, educated generations of social workers, many of whom are here tonight. Their teaching will endure long after the curriculum committees have buried themselves. In their tradition, that of the great teachers, everything that is important in education takes place within the relationship of a teacher and a student. It is a melancholy fact that no professional conference has ever been convened to praise the curriculum that gave credentials, or the curriculum committee that created the edifice, brick by brick. All that is preserved in memory are a few unforgettable teachers, and their teaching, and so it happens that meetings such as this are convened to honor our teachers and to ask ourselves, as teachers, what it is that we value and want to entrust to a new generation of social workers.

REFERENCES

Adelson, E., and Fraiberg, S. An Abandoned Mother, An Abandoned Baby, *Menninger Bulletin*, 1977, 41(2), 162–180.

Fraiberg, S., Adelson, E., and Shapiro, V. Ghosts in the Nursery: A Psychoanalytic Approach to the Problems of the Impaired Infant-Mother Relationships, *The Journal of the American Academy of Child Psychiatry*, 1975, 14(3), 287–421.

Fraiberg, S. Applications of Psychoanalytic Principles in Casework Practice with Children, *Quarterly Journal of Child Behavior*, 1951.

Fraiberg, S. Teaching Psychoanalytic Theory to Social Work Students, *Social Casework*, June, 1955.

Fraiberg, S. *Psychoanalytic Principles in Casework with Children*. New York: Family Service Association of America. Pamphlet, 1954, 54 pp.

Shapiro, V., Fraiberg, S. and Adelson, E. Infant-Parent Psychotherapy on Behalf of a Child in a Critical Nutritional State, *Psychoanalytic Study of the Child*, 1976, 31, 463–93.

Part Two
ADULTS

MARY L. GOTTESFELD

5

The Invited Guest in a Mother's Therapy: Fostering Symbolic Recapitulation of Developmental Conflict

THE PRESENCE of significant others in the therapy room in addition to the acknowledged patient is not an unusual occurrence. In fact, it was this practice that perhaps culminated formally in group and family therapy. Although the therapy room is sacrosanct for the person in therapy if confidentiality is to be maintained, clients will bring into therapy persons or objects that are important to them. For example, a child will bring siblings or friends, or a mother will bring her baby, other children, or spouse, without asking. Introducing the other person into treatment often is an expression of the client's separation difficulties, and understanding the need for the person's presence can be a valuable piece of therapeutic work.

The therapist usually does not invite someone into the client's therapy, of course. In the case reported here, however, the therapist suggested to a new mother who was unable to separate from her infant that she bring the baby to therapy.

Mrs. A., age 27, had been married for three years when she sought therapy. One reason was her inability to conceive a child. She had a master's degree in business administration and worked as an executive in a large corporation. She did not particularly like her job and was unhappy with her choice of career, which added to her frustration about not achieving a desired pregnancy. She was the youngest of four children; all her siblings were boys. Her father's family came from an Islamic country, and her mother was from eastern Europe. While growing up, she had to cater to her brothers as her mother catered to her father: for example, she had to make their beds, clean their rooms, and help her mother wash, iron, and cook for them. She was always aware of her mother's unhappiness about being at home. For financial reasons, her mother began working as a saleswoman when the patient was 6 years old and was relatively successful. When Mrs. A. reached adulthood, her mother confirmed how unhappy she had been before she began working.

Mrs. A. supported herself through college with scholarships and summer jobs. She also lived abroad for a year on her own, then returned and obtained her M.B.A. with the help of educational loans. She met her husband-to-be in graduate school, and they married soon after graduation. Her husband was a research scientist who spent long hours at work and was socially rather isolated.

DIAGNOSIS AND TREATMENT

Mrs. A. was an attractive, neatly groomed woman with little emotional expression and a somewhat angry, yet depressed, look. During an unusually brief (five-minute) consultation interview, she complained of general unhappiness, which she related to her dissatisfaction with her job and her failure to become pregnant, and also mentioned a "problem with authorities." She concluded the interview by asking if the therapist would treat her, and she arranged for twice-weekly sessions.

As therapy progressed it became obvious that Mrs. A. was extremely angry, and she developed a negative, or narcissistic transference (Spotnitz, 1978; Spotnitz and Meadow, 1976). She seemed somewhat lethargic and said she retired early at night. She was also hypersensitive, perceiving most of the therapist's remarks as attacking or hostile. As a result, there was little interaction between them, and Mrs. A. was extremely angry about it.

The client's history and level of affective functioning pointed to developmental failure, and she was diagnosed as having a narcissistic personality disorder—her pathology was based on her internal, emotional state (autoplastic symptoms) rather than on external conflicts, as characterized by narcissistic behavior disorders (in which alloplastic symptoms such as delinquency or addiction predominate) (Kohut, 1972). As mentioned earlier, Mrs. A. was depressed, lethargic, and hypersensitive. Kohut and Wolf (1978) describe "contact shunning personalities" as follows:

Although for obvious reasons they attract the least notice, they may well be the most frequent of the narcissistic character types. These individuals avoid social contact and become isolated, not because they are disinterested in others, but, on the contrary, just because their need for them is so intense. The intensity of their need not only leads to great sensitivity to rejection— a sensitivity of which they are painfully aware—but also, on deeper and unconscious levels, to the apprehension that the remnants of their nuclear self will be swallowed up and destroyed by the yearned for all-encompassing union (p. 422).

The concept of the narcissistic transference flows naturally from an understanding of clients with preverbal disorders; that is, fixations within the first two years of life. The traditional view that analysis required a working alliance with the therapist, and that consequently clients needed mature egoes to express verbally the conflicts creating their symptoms within the context of transference and resistance, had to be abandoned when working with individuals who demonstrated preoedipal patterns. In the proper therapeutic environment these clients will regress and reexperience feelings that mirror a time in the past when their maturation was impeded by the mothering person. When this emotional level predates verbal communication, the transference is not an object transference but a narcissistic transference. Spotnitz (1976), a pioneer in enlarging Freud's concepts to encompass the narcissistic disorders, states that:

In a negative, regressed state, the patient may experience the analyst as being like him or a part of him. Or the analyst may not exist for him. The syntonic feeling of oneness is a curative one, while the feeling of aloneness, the withdrawn state, is merely protective. Because traces of narcissism remain in everyone, we seek, when beginning treatment, to create an environment that will facilitate a narcissistic transference so that, first, we can work through the patient's narcissistic aggression. The extent to which the patient wards us off and avoids emotional contact tells us the degree to which he is narcissistically fixated. He will gradually increase his contacts with us if we create the appropriate environment. To establish the ego-syntonic atmosphere in which the patient can view us as being like him, or at least non-threatening and non-judgmental, modern analysts carefully avoid exposing the patient to any uninvited communication or interpretation. When the patient feels that he can say and feel things without taking action, his emotional contacts with the analyst will increase (p. 67).

Toward the end of the first year of therapy, Mrs. A. became pregnant. Although pleased, she felt nauseated and vomited. Following her analysis midway through the pregnancy that she perceived the fetus as being like herself—unwanted and therefore bad—her physical symptoms abated somewhat but persisted throughout the pregnancy. After an uncomplicated delivery, she gave birth to a daughter.

By previous agreement, the client returned to therapy a month after the baby was born, announcing that she had come only because her husband had stayed home with the baby. She said she would have to discontinue therapy for the time being because she was unable to arrange for a babysitter. (Since Mrs. A. lived in à development where many young mothers lived, and it was near the therapist's office, the therapist knew this was not a real problem.) The therapist inquired about the baby and learned that she was being breastfed and was an active but easy child. Then Mrs. A. said that she had gone to a pediatrician the previous week for the first time. After examining the child, the physician told her to follow him into his office for some instructions while the nurse dressed and diapered the baby in the examining room. Mrs. A. reported that she became hysterical and could not leave the baby and follow the physician, who berated her for being a "crazy mother." At that point Mrs. A. picked up the child and left his office. She then repeated that babysitting arrangements were impossible and that she would have to stop therapy for an indefinite period.

At this point the therapist suggested that Mrs. A. bring the baby with her until she could make satisfactory babysitting arrangements. Mrs. A. was pleased, and for the next three weeks the baby attended her therapy sessions, lying contentedly in a bassinet on the floor near her mother. After three weeks Mrs. A. arranged for a sitter and left the baby at home. When a second child was born three years later, she experienced no similar difficulties.

THEORETICAL BASIS FOR INTERVENTION

When her first baby was born, Mrs. A. had been in therapy for 18 months and her own conflicts about individuation had begun to emerge. These conflicts primarily concerned her fear of being close and her wish for closeness and merger, which would result again in the rejection she felt from her own mother. Her feelings about closeness and fusion were reactivated even more powerfully because her own infant was in a state of symbiotic fusion with her. (The client's ambivalence about conception and pregnancy and her view of herself as the bad fetus were mentioned earlier.) Now she was also the infant who wished for merger, not withdrawal; consequently, she had been unable to separate from her child.

Realizing that a symbolic recapitulation of Mrs. A.'s development conflict was occurring, the therapist felt that a more idealized parent–child relationship could take place in therapy. By inviting Mrs. A. to bring the infant to her sessions, the therapist communicated acceptance, not rejection and premature separation, and a powerful opportunity for establishment of basic trust was created.

Narcissistic clients do not communicate their feelings and, in fact, often act as though the therapist were not there. Because they fear entrusting themselves to another person, they, like Mrs. A., often give the appearance of great independence and self-sufficiency. This behavior, however, masks their conflict over individuation and the disruption of the illusionary wish for merger. The therapeutic value of such a metaphorical replay from early distortion of object relations has been observed by several prominent analysts (Balint, 1968; Nelson, 1968; Spotnitz, 1978; Winnicott, 1965), who point out the potential for a new object tie with the therapist. Modell (1979) uses Winnicott's term "holding environment" to describe the analytic situation that permits symbolic recreation of early developmental conflicts and suggests "something more: that it is possible to re-create symbolically an earlier developmental period and to provide a measure of actual gratification" (p. 495). In Mrs. A.'s case the therapist/mother communicated acceptance of the client/daughter(s), and thus not only permitted but welcomed symbiotic merger, normal for the emotional period. When the client was satiated and could trust the therapist's acceptance as genuine, she communicated this to the therapist by obtaining a babysitter.

EPILOGUE

Many clinicians have ably put into practice programs that are based on early object relations theory [e.g., see Holman (1980) based on Mahler (1968)]. These programs have been developed to meet the needs of children, not mothers. But, as Mrs. A. illustrates, the reverse can also be true, on the basis of that same theory. Yet one might ask whether there is any effect on the infant in these cases. An unanswerable question, perhaps, given the infant's perceptual ability at an early age. Nevertheless, a comment that Mrs. A. made to the therapist three years later is interesting:

I was sitting down and browsing through a book that you had coauthored, and my daughter (then 3 years old) came over, pointed to your photograph on the book jacket, and said, "My friend, my friend."

REFERENCES

Balint, M. *The Basic Fault: Therapeutic Aspects of Regression*. London, Tavistock, 1968.

Holman, S. An Early Intervention Program for Developmentally At-Risk Toddlers and Their Mothers. *Clinical Social Work Journal* 1980, 8, 1.

Kohut, H. *The Restoration of the Self*. New York: International Universities Press, 1972.

Kohut, H., and Wolf, E. The Disorders of the Self and Their Treatment: An Outline. *International Journal of Psycho-Analysis*, 1978, 59, 3–425.

Mahler, M. *On Human Symbiosis and the Vicissitudes of Individuation*. Vol. 1. New York: International Universities Press, 1968.

Modell, A. The Conceptualization of the Therapeutic Action of Psychoanalysis: The Action of the Holding Environment. *Bulletin of the Minninger Clinic*, 1979, 42(6), 493–504.

Nelson, M. C., et al. *Roles and Paradigms in Psychotherapy*. New York: Grune & Stratton, 1968.

Spotnitz, H. *Psychotherapy for Pre-oedipal Disorders*. New York: Jason Aronson, 1978.

Spotnitz, H., and Meadow, P. *Treatment of the Narcissistic Neuroses*. New York: Modern Psychoanalytic Publications, 1976.

Winnicott, D. *The Maturational Process and the Facilitating Environment*. New York: International Universities Press, 1965.

TERRY DE GROOT

6

Reparation After the Countertransference

Two prisoners in contingent cells, who communicate by blows struck on the wall. The wall is what separates them but also what permits them to communicate...Every separation is a bond.
  (Simone Weil as quoted by May Sarton, *The Small Room*).

The bond of separation is the outcome of the satisfactory development of object relations and a desirable result of the therapeutic process. Unresolved internal problems in either the mother or the therapist can lead to disruption of the appropriate bonding and separation processes necessary for optimal growth and development. Countertransference has been discussed in the literature from many viewpoints (Epstein and Feiner, 1979, Chedicak, 1979, Racker, 1957, Sandler, Dare, and Holder, 1973) but less attention has been paid to the need for reparation after the countertransference. This chapter discusses the positive contributions of reparation to therapeutic progress.

BOND OF SEPARATION

Libidinal object constancy is the internalized bond that is achieved in part through the particular structure the mother brings to the separation–individuation process. The developmental bond

79

of separation is seen in the young toddler's "looking back at his mother and moving on." The very act of looking back is an acknowledgement of the bond, and vice versa. Neither process can be carried out well enough unless the mother helps by providing for *both herself and her child* a structure that will facilitate the child's ability to move on *because* the mother has allowed for it. This structure (Weil's necessary wall) is the mother's special availability to her child, complemented by her availability to herself, that is, her monitoring of her own separate inner and outer life.

Progress from dependence toward independence, in Winnicott's view (1965), can only be accomplished "by continuous management by a human being who is consistently herself...; what the infant needs is just what he usually gets, the care and attention of someone who is going on being herself" (pp. 87–88). The mother's particular structure thus provides the infant/child with a consistent boundary to act and react to (an available mother whom the child cannot destroy because she in reality prevents destruction by going on being herself), enabling separation to take place. It is a structure that holds both mother and child and one that wavers and falters—but does not collapse—under the demands of the developmental process.

The good-enough mother's own self-development does not come to a halt so that she can provide optimal care-taking. Good-enough mothering implies that the mother's continued growth will synchronize with her child's growth. For example, a client of average intelligence who had barely completed high school told her therapist about the following experience with her young daughter. While watching the child play, she began to wonder about thinking, about how ideas happen, about the self that is seen and the self that is felt. She was delighted with the "creation" of her questions and wanted to know from her therapist what she had stumbled onto. Could she learn more about it? Were there books to read? Could she take a course?

The mother's particular stucture is a continuous contribution toward the establishment and keeping of the holding environment, where the reevolving bond of separation takes place. Out of proper bonding comes proper separation, and out of proper separation comes proper bonding. These processes must work in tandem if they are to be developed satisfactorily.

Mahler (1972) sees "the entire life cycle as constituting a more or less successful process of distancing from and introjection of the lost symbiotic mother..." (p. 338). Her names for the three separation–individuation subphases—differentiation, practicing, rapprochement—illustrate this process, which can be carried out only within the context of the idea of coming together, then apart, then together, then apart, again and again. The ability to build on the one depends on the presence of the other, within a holding environment that moves according to the cohesiveness of the mother's particular structure and the quality of her "failures."

According to Winnicott (1965), during the period of relative dependence the baby begins to experience the mother's "gradual failure of adaptation" (p. 87); for example, her failure to present the bottle immediately to an older infant. Her failures start to appear when the baby is ready to use maturationally increasing cognitive and physical resources to organize its inner world and adapt creatively to the loss of her "primary maternal preoccupation," that of bringing the baby its bottle—its mother—on time. In Khan's words (1964):

The inevitable temporary failures of the mother as protective shield are not only corrected and recovered from in the evolving complexity and articulation of the maturational process, but they also provide nutriment and stimulus to new functions in growth and mastery of the environment (p. 61).

The ability to fail gradually depends on the mother's state of mental well-being. If her own life is empty or chaotic or if she is needy, anxious, or easily thrown by loss or narcissistic blows, she loses her ability to provide this supportive structure with its appropriate failures that enable her child to develop its own separate self. She is a mother who is not going on being herself, and therefore can be felt by the child as being "destroyed" through the expression of the child's needs. Even temporary losses of the structure can cause constricting states of developmental failure.

FAILURE AS PROTECTIVE SHIELD

In "The Concept of Cumulative Trauma" Khan (1963) describes the pathogenic build-up of ego deficits that occurs in the child when the mother fails as a protective shield—whenever she is unable to be "alert, adaptive, and organizing."

It is the intrusion of her personal needs and conflicts that I characterize as her failure in respect of her role as a protective shield...The protective-shield role is the result of conflict-free autonomous ego-functions in the mother. If personal conflicts intrude here, the result is a shift from the protective-shield role to that of symbiosis or rejective withdrawal (p. 50).

Case Example

The intense rage, envy, and loss of self experienced by Mr. A., a client who transferred into private treatment with his therapist after she left a clinic setting, illustrates the effects of this type of failure. At the clinic Mr. A. had viewed the therapist as "clinic issue"—not only as not having her own separate life, but as being almost part and parcel of the clinic, as the furniture there had been. His feelings about being forced to "see" her in a new setting, one that was obviously her own creation, became more understandable when they were related to his mother's intense difficulties concerning his early separation activities. One result then was that he had developed a severe skin disease, which hampered his autonomous physical functioning and which his mother ascribed as an allergy to his playing outdoors, especially in "dirt" and away from her.

Later, when his mother began to develop interests of her own, Mr. A. responded with intense rage, envy, and feelings of desertion. His mother became fearful, guilt-ridden, and angry about his reactions, and he in turn became fearful and angry about hers. The result was a kind of choreography in which each seemingly became envious, immobilized, and destructive when confronted with any manifestation of a separate life in the other.

Out of the clinical experience come illustrations of the therapist's particular structure, which is his or her continuous contribution toward the establishment and keeping of the therapeutic holding environment. In a discussion about this environment Modell (1976) describes the therapist as follows:

The analyst is constant and reliable; he responds to the patient's affects; he accepts the patient and his judgement is less critical and more benign; he is there primarily for the patient's needs and not for his own; he does not retaliate; and he does at time have a better grasp of the patient's psychic reality than does the patient himself and therefore may clarify what is bewildering and confusing. (p. 291).

Winnicott (1965) referred to the "professional attitude," which *"assumes a distance between analyst and patient"* and contains the analyst's "technique, the work he does with his mind" (p. 161). The professional attitude is being viewed here as the therapist's particular structure (Weil's necessary wall), one that is akin to the mother's. It is an ever-present state of being with the client and is composed of the known quality of the therapist's normal working stance together with the therapist's known usual way of responding to the ordinary reverberations of the client. Stance is this sense means the therapists' knowledge of what they are like usually with all clients: their style, posture, gestures; how they listen, react, respond; how they use themselves; how they suspend their personal lives while working. The term reverberation refers to their knowledge of how they usually respond to each client: how they react to that client as a person—to the client's character style, self-presentation, methods of engagement and disengagement, history, and current living situation; how they feel about the client; who the client is for them.

This particular structure provides the client with a consistent boundary to act and react to (an available therapist whom the client cannot destroy because the therapist in reality prevents destruction by going on being him- or herself) and thus enables the therapeutic process to take place. This structure is also one that wavers and falters and one that will eventually become a product of both participants' combined efforts to keep the therapeutic process going. Clients give their therapists excellent supervision in order to maintain the wall; for example, by saying, "You keep asking me if I'm angry with you. But it's like how can you be angry with the only mother you've got?" Or by bringing the therapist a Christmas gift of narcissus bulbs.

SHIFT IN THE STRUCTURE—COUNTERTRANSFERENCE

The therapist, like the mother, will fail, gradually and appropriately, and these failures will be incorporated into the working and therapeutic alliances. The concept of countertransference enters into the therapist's felt shifting of this structure (when the therapist's working stance alters, or responses to a client change). Both therapist and client experience a loss of synchronization, and the holding environment takes on a new dimension; the treatment either will become impeded or enhanced and forwarded, the outcome depending to a great degree on the therapist's state of mental well-being and skill in supervising the countertransference.

Countertransference is seen here as the recognition and corraling of a runaway shift in the therapist's structure. Shifts are inherent in the life of the treatment process, and if there is no recognition of them, there is, in a sense, no countertransference, only checkmated therapy. (This broad view also helps to distinguish between idiosyncratic and inevitable countertransference.) The reason for the shift in the structure may result from the therapist's transference to the client, countertransference to the client's transference, intrusion of personal stresses, or empathic identification. Self-analysis, supervision, or personal analysis will enable the therapist to untangle the reasons.

What is important is that a shift in the structure—a breach in the wall—has taken place. There has been another kind of failure, one not accounted for in its enactment by the therapist's involvement in his or her own or the client's growth; the process of proper bonding and separation has been disrupted. Khan (1964) referred to impingements resulting from the mother's failure as a protective shield, which "start a process of interplay with the mother and environment which not only interferes with the mother's adaptation to the infant but also [has] fateful consequences for the emergent ego-formation..." (p. 61).

It is in the therapist's understanding of these shifts that the structure is improved upon, and it is in working through the countertransference with the client that their relationship is strengthened and the client is given the opportunity to renew his or her interest in an object-related world. The therapists learn more about themselves and their clients, thus increasing their capacity to be available to both and enabling greater bonding and separation to take place. They learn to be attentive to the shifts that the structure reflects, to adjust again and again to varying degrees of therapeutic closeness and distance required during these shifts. They monitor objective love as well as objective hate, subjective love and subjective hate, objective and subjective curiosity, and use of self and ego ideals. Experiences of countertransference can be described as positive or negative, helpful or unhelpful, but never as good or bad.

REPARATION

The literature contains many good articles on countertransference that cover historical overviews, discuss the fluctuations of interest in the subject, and thoughtfully probe into its uses and abuses. Here the focus will be the idea of reparation in countertransference.

According to Khan (1964), in reparation:

There exists a profound urge to make sacrifices in order to help and to put right loved people who have in phantasy been harmed or destroyed...To be genuinely considerate implies that we can put ourselves in the place of other people...in being identified with other people we share, as it were, the help or satisfaction afforded to them by ourselves, [and] we regain in one way what we have sacrificed in another...This *making reparation* is...a fundamental element in love and in all human relationships (p. 65-68).

In Winnicott's view (1965) reparation develops from the capacity for concern: "The individual *cares*, or *minds*, and both feels and accepts responsibility" (p. 73).

When the structure shifts so that the therapist is in the client's way, reparation is in order. The therapist *needs* to make reparation, for his or her well-being and for the client's. Although clinical errors often become serendipitous in the forwarding of treatment, the act of reparation—because of the therapist's need and the client's response—can be a less than comfortable one for the therapist, both in fantasy and in reality. This may create a subsequent wish to deny future countertransferential shifts, either with a particular client or the same kind of shift with any client.

Because reparation involves two people, there will be issues to consider on both sides. For the therapist, it is important to be aware of what such an experience usually is like. The therapist must also consider how he or she feels about indicating to this particular client that an error has been made (and if in supervision, to the supervisor as well), and will have to prevent him- or herself from acting out a wish for the client to accept a reparative gesture.

The therapist's method of working through the error with the client will not include a discussion about the therapist's psyche. The reparative gesture may range from a simple reshifting in the session to acknowledging with the client that something unusual has taken place. Such validation *is* the client's business; the content, however, can be burdensome and should be discussed sparingly and judiciously, if at all. For instance, acknowledgment might include a thoughtful formulation of why the error occurred within the therapeutic relationship; it would never include words that imply the patient was bad, manipulative, seductive, at fault, or in any way responsible for the therapist's action.

CONFIRMATION AND ACCEPTANCE; DISCONFIRMATION

In the client's experience reparation appears to be a two-part process of *confirming* the gesture within the relationship and of *accepting* the gesture internally; that is, trusting it as a genuine attempt to put things right and discovering what that restitution brings to the self. Accepting the reparative gesture internally may take a long time. (One client took four years to forgive her therapist internally for taking a vacation during the first year they worked together.) The therapist must wait skillfully: internal acceptance can neither be rushed nor neglected, and the client is in complete charge of the process of allowing him- or herself to be put right.

The larger difficulty, then, is disconfirmation of the reparative gesture within the relationship, of the therapist's acknowledgment that he or she has somehow disrupted the process and thus the relationship. According to Watzlawick et al. (1967, p. 86), "While rejection amounts to the message 'You are wrong,' disconfirmation says in effect 'You do not exist.' " They quote Laing's view that:

When no matter how a person feels or acts, no matter what meaning he gives his situation, his feelings are denuded of validity, his acts are stripped of their motives, intentions, consequences, the situation is robbed of its meaning for him so that he is totally mystified and alienated (p. 87).

Case Example

Mr. A. illustrated the phenomenon of disconfirmation when his therapist, because of an unexpected change in her personal life, told him that she would have to cancel as many as one third of their sessions over a two-month period. The timing was particularly regrettable because it occurred after a major holiday and just before Mr. A.'s vacation, and the sessions could not be rescheduled. The therapist knew that merely telling Mr. A. about these interruptions would disrupt their relationship on many levels. And she knew that he knew it. Yet Mr. A., who was usually articulate about his feelings of anger and abandonment, said it was fine and countered the therapist's focus on the disruption by thanking her for giving him notice. All of the therapist's further attempts at exploration were met by Mr. A.'s increasingly polite verbal brushoffs. The therapist began to feel that the therapy was somehow unimportant to him—that she only imagined they had a good working alliance, that there was something wrong with her perceptions. After a long silence, she recovered her equilibrium and casually mentioned to him that he was not permitting her any form of reparation. Apparently this comment collided sufficiently with the "good" image he felt he was presenting, and they were able to talk about his need to regain control over her by dismissing her efforts to discuss the matter. Mr.

A.'s mother had repeatedly responded this way to him during his attempts at reparation after bouts of rage with her.

If clients can discuss their feelings about an original disruption or a current gesture of reparation, if they can respond to the therapist's reshifting of the structure or are able to hear usefully the therapist saying, "I made an error; I'm sorry," then the therapy can continue, even if they have not accepted the reparation internally. Confirmation and acceptance of reparation do not imply positive effect on a client's part. What is important is the emergence of *real* feelings, whatever their form and content.

When a client does not confirm the reparative gesture, the therapist should pay attention to the need to refuse it. Although Winnicott (1965) cautions this from a developmental context, his remarks are relevant here in understanding an aspect of withdrawal on the therapist's part: "If there is [no one] to receive the reparative gesture, the guilt becomes intolerable, and concern cannot be felt. Failure of reparation leads to a losing of the capacity for concern..." (p. 82).

Case Example

Mrs. V. was in individual therapy with a female therapist and in a group led by her therapist and a male colleague. During a group session the male therapist misunderstood a request of Mrs. V.'s and thus failed to respond as she expected. This "broken promise" came to light during a later session when the other group members said they had heard Mrs. V.'s original request. The cotherapist said he wanted to think privately about why he had misunderstood Mrs. V., but he apologized for his error. Mrs. V. responded by becoming silent, drying an occasional tear; the room's atmosphere felt frozen. Because her response was one of accusation ("I've got you") rather than a confirmation of his reparative gesture, Mrs. V. kept him both at bay and on the hook and did not free him for other work. Consequently, the group could neither move on to someone else nor release the therapist from being "bad."

The female therapist suddenly recalled a puzzling incident that Mrs. V. had reported to her earlier. Mr. V. had confessed to his wife that he was having an affair but expressed a deep wish to continue their marriage. Several weeks later, he erupted angrily, saying he couldn't stand it any longer and wanted a divorce. At the time Mrs. V. and the therapist had been mystified by what he meant by "it." During the group session Mrs. V. talked about not wanting the cotherapist to make reparation. She was able to make the connection between the current incident and the reaction of her husband and others who had ended their relationships with her. Mrs. V. said that not permitting the other person to say he had been wrong or hurtful made her feel in control and strong. However, she had always felt even more injured when the other person subsequently moved out of her life. These relationships eventually eroded because the other person had to take himself off the hook (since Mrs. V. would not do it) and could do so only by disengagement and withdrawal.

CONCLUSION

Both mother and therapist bring particular structures to their holding environments. These structures are alike in the sense that for optimal development to take place, each requires a highly sensitive availability to the child or client and sensitive monitoring of each one's own inner states. These structures permit internalized bonding and separation—separation and bonding to occur because the mother and therapist go on being themselves to allow for the variations of need inherent in development. Countertransference is viewed as any shift in the therapist's structure, and the therapist must make reparation after recognizing that he or she has interrupted the therapeutic process and relationship. Reparation for the client is a two-part process, of confirmation and then acceptance of the geture. One difficult aspect of the reparative process is the client's disconfirmation of the therapist's reparative gesture, which should be given careful attention if it appears.

REFERENCES

Chediak, C. Counteractions and Countertransference. *The International Journal of Psycho-Analysis*, 1979, 60, 117-129.

Epstein, L., and Feiner, A. H. Countertransference: The Therapist's Contribution to Treatment. *Contemporary Psychoanalysis*, 1979, 15, 489–513.

Khan, M. R. The Concept of Cumulative Trauma. In *The Privacy of the Self.* New York: International Universities Press, 1963, pp. 420–458.

Khan, M. R. Ego-Distortion, Cumulative Trauma in the Role of Reconstruction in the Analytic Situation. In *The Privacy of the Self.* New York: International Universities Press, 1964, pp. 59–68.

Mahler, M. On the First Three Subphases of the Separation–Individuation Process. *International Journal of Psycho-Analysis*, 1972, 53, 333–338.

Modell, A. H. The Holding Environment and the Therapeutic Action of Psychoanalysis. *Journal of the American Psychoanalytic Association*, 1976, 24, 285–307.

Racker, H. *Transference and Countertransference.* New York: International Universities Press, 1957.

Sandler, J., Dare, C., and Holder, A. *The Patient and the Analyst.* New York: International Universities Press, 1973.

Watzlawick, P., Beavin, J., and Jackson, D. *Pragmatics of Human Communication.* New York: W.W. Norton, 1967.

Winnicott, D. W. *The Maturational Process and the Facilitating Environment.* New York: International Universities Press, 1965.

ELSIE HERMAN

7

Marital Couples in Stress: Therapeutic Strategy

THIS CHAPTER DISCUSSES "marital therapy," defined as the application of any planned therapeutic techniques within the context of individual and/or conjoint and/or group modalities to modify maladaptive interactions and transactions of couples in a committed sexual relationship. The critical content of the study-assessment and engagement phase of intervention is explicated as the criteria for choice of therapeutic strategy.

Marital conflict is the major problem with which human relations workers wrestle (Beck and Jones, 1973, p. 36). Divorce statistics attest to the gargantuan percentage of marriages that are aborted. They do not begin to reflect the number of marriages that continue with families locked in pain.

Literature dealing with marital conflict offers a rich array of approaches (e.g., Ackerman, 1967; Blanck and Blanck, 1688; Kempler, 1975; Lederer and Jackson, 1968; Markowitz and Kadis, 1968; Satir, 1967). The techniques are usually insight, problem-solving, or behaviorally oriented with the frameworks of analytic ego psychology, learning, general systems, and communications theories. All of these approaches assume specific focal target areas and a particular modality. Although indications and contraindications for one or another specific approach have been advanced (e.g., Boszormenyi-Nagy, 1969; Walrond-Skinner, 1977), there is little in the literature that speaks to the criteria to be weighed in the *choice* among the many possible strategies.

RATIONALE FOR STUDY ASSESSMENT

Omission of the study-assessment process is partner to indiscriminate, often rigid treatment strategy. Although the confidence of the therapist subscribing to one preset therapeutic strategy initially may foster corresponding hope, a necessary ingredient for client engagement, hope usually can be rendered more realistically. The hazards to be weighed against a recipe strategy are minimal or zero therapeutic gain and discouraged withdrawal by client or therapist, frequently reasoned by the therapist as lack of client motivation. At worst, clients may suffer negative consequences beyond the loss of time and money.

The formal or informal policy of a social agency or practitioner following one or another theoretical stance, exclusive of all others, may dictate, for example, that a couple that goes to agency A may never be seen by the therapist(s) in a conjoint interview, whereas the couple that attends clinic B may never be offered the opportunity to speak with the therapist apart from the marital partner.

The practice of agency A may be based solely on psychoanalytic developmental theory that views marital conflict as a consequence primarily of intrapsychic conflict and of each individual's stage of development. Thus individual insight-oriented therapy for each partner, preferably with separate therapists, may be predicated, although the therapist "sometimes yields to the wishes of the spouse that they be seen together in the beginning, because this is the only way in which they can begin, but is always mindful that it is usually more desirable for them to have separate counselors" (Blanck and Blanck, 1968, p. 165).

On the other hand, the practice of clinic B, which may be based on systems and learning theory, may view marital conflict as a systemic property to be alleviated through the realignment of positions vis-à-vis the couple, or the entire family, and the conjoint practice of new behaviors and improved communication (Lederer and Jackson, 1968; Satir, 1967). In fact, if practitioners strictly follow the principles of some family therapy theorists, study of the client's previous life experience for understanding of the current attitudes and functioning is considered contraindicated. "The family therapist does not need to collect a 'history' before he can proceed to offer treatment; he has before him the most significant gestalt of all, the current interactions...of the family members in the here and now of the therapy sessions..."(Walrond-Skinner, 1977,

p. 38). It is in accordance with this approach that all family members are invited to attend treatment conjointly from the first interview onward, and individual contacts with the therapists are discouraged. It must be emphasized that all family therapists do not subscribe to this implied rigidity, at least after the initial interviews (Haley, 1971).

MARRIAGE STATUS

Individuals come together for positive satisfactions, which include feelings of significance, stimulation, security, and connectedness. They sometimes stay together, even when there is not much positive satisfaction, for reasons of guilt, neurotic compulsion, or fear of being alone, unrelated, and inadequate to meet their emotional and physical needs. In choosing target areas and setting realistic outcome goals, the following topology has been found useful for defining the status of the marriage.

In a *pre-stable* marriage new partners are learning about each other and what it is like to live together, with their primary task to clarify and negotiate their mutual expectations. Involvement and commitment to the relationship may be shallow if need satisfaction has been the primary reason for the marriage. Marital counseling may be sought when they have difficult negotiating differences relating to both conscious and unconscious expectations and to each individual's bonding requirements (physical and emotional nexus). In seeking counseling the goal of one or both may be marital stabilization or dissolution.

A *pseudo-stable* marriage may have some positive satisfactions, but one or both partners have frequently contemplated divorce and have discontentedly maintained the relationship for a combination of negative reasons. These reasons may include a conflict of conscious and unconscious desires. Counseling may be sought when the balance of the relationship has undergone change, upsetting intrapsychic equilibrium of one or both partners, and there is the wish to return to the old balance or to work through to dissolution.

A *stable* marriage is one in which there is a good enough fit of expectations and bonding requirements. In the balance the relationship is maintained more because of positive satisfactions of both partners rather than out of guilt or fear of consequences of dissolution of the marriage, although the degree of common interests, sexual excitement, respect, and empathy may vary considerably from couple to couple. One or both partners may seek marital counseling in an effort to restabilize a relationship that has gone negatively askew with unusual stress that is felt as a threat to the marriage.

An *unstable* marriage is one that was formerly stable or pseudo-stable but has been thrown off balance by trauma or significant change.

It is important to compare the present marriage status with what it has been. Although individuals may cite a long-standing grievance, for example, lack of communication, or dwell on much-suffered problem behavior such as alcoholism, it is necessary to discern what, in fact, has triggered the request for service *at this time*. What is the area or overlapping areas of trauma and/or change that may have acted as disequilibrator to upset the balance necessary to one or both individuals for maintenance of the relationship? It cannot be assumed that for each individual the initial goal of therapy is a stable marriage. Individuals may be seeking an old pseudo-stable balance or, indeed, it may be determined that one or both of the partners have already largely decathected from their relationship and are asking for separation rather than marital counseling.

COMMON DISEQUILIBRATORS

The disequilibrator can be the marriage itself, in which individual equilibrium has been upset by the entrance into a committed relationship with one or more persons (merging families). An ongoing, widened field of self-reference is entailed, as is the negotiation of complex and sometimes conflicting conscious and unconscious expectations in a thrust toward stabilization of the relationship. Individuals often are faced with a reality that runs counter to fantasies. Sexual fears and taboos may erupt.

• Developmental family changes such as addition of children demand learning and accommodation to the new roles of parenthood and changed expectations of marital partners. Old sibling rivalries and feelings of displacement may be aroused and played out in various ways. Adolescence of children, whicch is characterized by marked movement into adult sexuality and separation–individuation, calls for reciprocal adjustments in the parenting roles with possible repercussions on the marital relationship. There may be arousal of taboo areas of sexuality in one or both partners with fear of loss of control, as well as feelings of grief and loss related to their own youth. Anxiety associated with middle age and the need for self-confirmation may be acted out in extramarital relations, or in the decision to dissolve the marriage to be free for new, more exciting relationships. Departure of children may be felt as complete loss of the parental role and set into motion a grieving process, with possible depression of one or both partners. Submerged areas of marital conflict may surface in the absence of a child or children who might have previously carried the burden of the conflict.

• Individual developmental change may occur as a consequence of successful entrance into new roles and social systems, for example, vocational or avocational. Self-image may be enhanced and role expectations altered. A resultant marked shift in behavior pattern may seriously impact the marital relationship. For instance, the lessening of dependency in one spouse may catalyze an escalation of anxiety and unmasking of dependency in the other. This dependency may further alienate the first spouse struggling to work through separation–individuation. Aging, with its physical problems, losses, and increased dependencies, may also initiate physical and/or emotional withdrawal by one or both partners.

• Chronic impairment or death of a child with resultant grief that may not have been worked through individually or together may lead to depression of one or both partners or displacement of guilt and anger on each other.

• Chronic disability or life-threatening illness of spouse may involve a difficult shift in role expectations and/or drastic loss of security. Grieving may occur with concomitant emotional estrangement.

• Change or loss of roles in significant social systems (other than the nuclear family), such as job change, retirement from vocation, or even moving to another city or neighborhood, may necessitate a difficult renegotiation of mutual expectations. Stress may be expressed through symptomatic behavior that impacts the marriage. The self-image of one or both partners may be negatively affected, with resultant depression and withdrawal in the sexual as well as other areas.

• Partner substitution may occur when the marriage has been pseudo-stable in order to facilitate separation from the spouse. When one person has effected cathexis to a substitute, a desire for separation counseling to work through guilt or residual fears may underly the request for marital treatment.

Along with identification of the disequilibrators, there must be knowledge of the arena in which they operate, that is, of current marital system functioning related to each individual's own dynamics.

SYSTEM FUNCTIONING

The pattern of the partners' transactions with each other must be understood to clarify the marital system. This includes the expression and negotiation of expectations and differences and the coping with loving as well as with anger and grief. The communication pattern will reflect the nature of defenses as well as symbiotic and transference elements.

Second, it is important to assess the pattern of the couple's transactions with other members of the family system to evaluate the boundaries of the marital conflict.

Third, there should be assessment of both individual and couple transactions with other significant social systems more fully to understand coping strengths and defenses, openness of the family system, and environmental supports.

For clarification of the transactional patterns and their purposes—that is, how they act to fill each individual's needs—there must be knowledge as far as possible of acculturation, values, self-expectations, self-image, object relations, ego strengths, and predominant ego defenses. Additionally, it is important to gain awareness of how each individual is related to the introjected historic family system. This relationship may be dysfunctionally played out in transference to current relationships, including relationship with the therapist. The view of the therapist will significantly influence motivation for engagement in the therapeutic endeavor.

MOTIVATION

Although a couple may request counseling to alleviate stress, the motivation of each person for therapeutic engagement may differ considerably. Motivation will depend on such variables as acculturation, feelings of investment, level of anxiety, fear of self-exposure, and fear of possible outcome. How these variables, as well as transference elements, are addressed in the initial counseling session may be crucial to whether individuals return for a second session.

Knowing who initiated the request for service and the attitudes of each partner regarding this request, as well as how the problem is individually defined and interpreted, will also provide clues to motivation and how it may be heightened to enable engagement.

PROCESS OF STUDY ASSESSMENT AND ENGAGEMENT

Because the study-assessment process is a mutual process, it is necessary to initiate engagement of each partner to assume the client role. This, of course, involves trust building in therapist understanding, acceptance, and competence, while allaying fears regarding the therapeutic venture.

Individual sessions with each partner *and* conjoint sessions with the couple are needed to fulfill all of the complex objectives of determining marriage status, disequilibrator(s), system functioning, and motivation in order to arrive at a therapeutic strategy. At least one family interview may be indicated if conflict is centered on or includes children or other family members with whom there is current, ongoing interaction, or if there seems to be a lack of role boundary between the couple and their kin.

When conjoint or family interviews are scheduled after there has already been an interview between the therapist and one family member, the relevant others should be given the same opportunity to know and be known by the therapist prior to the conjoint session(s). The possibility of the therapist being perceived as ally to one person over the other is thereby lessened. Usually, there is less hazard of discontinuance by potential clients if the intial contacts have been one to one, unless otherwise requested by the couple. In the individual session negative transference is more easily identified and addressed, as are differences such as age, sex, color, or race that might be perceived as a barrier to the therapist's understanding and acceptance. Ambivalence about therapy tied to fears and expectations is more accessible for exploration. Finally, the goals of each individual that are incongruent with goals of the other partner may be acknowledged more readily.

Secrets

In discussing engagement of the family in treatment, Walrond-Skinner (1977) states:

> For his part, the therapist must help the family to understand that whatever a family member shares with him he will consider to be the property of the whole group and share it with them. It is far better for the therapist to remain "in the dark" than to become privy to some highly charged private information about an individual which he cannot use, and which thus seriously hampers his spontaneity and freedom of movement in the session.

The spontaneity and freedom of movement of the client must be the primary consideration. In fashioning therapeutic strategy, the nature of the secret might, indeed, speak to the inadvisability of conjoint sessions as the primary modality, at least in the earlier stages of the therapeutic process. Often a partner's secret is crucially related to his/her conflict regarding continuance of the marriage, or hidden goal of marital dissolution. In the latter instance individual sessions may be necessary to enable conjoint discussion of disparate marital goals. Generally, however, in the interest of furthering therapeutic progress anything related by either partner may be considered open for discussion with both partners *unless* the information is red-tagged as confidential.

Therapeutic engagement does not occur until the formation of the therapeutic strategy. There must be agreement on the initial focal target areas, the context in which they will be addressed, that is, modality(ies), time frame, and, generally, the kind of techniques that will be used.

FORMATION OF THERAPEUTIC STRATEGY

Focal Target Areas

Choice of the initial focal target areas will be influenced by each partner's motivation and initial goals of therapeutic outcome. It should be related to the status of the marriage, and the disequilibrators as expressed within the context of the system functioning.

Case Example

Mr. and Mrs. Z., a white, childless couple in their late 30s, requested marital counseling after ten years of a chronically unhappy marriage. Although it held some positive satisfactions of security and relatedness, she in a childlike role and he as parent caretaker, it seemed to be glued together by her guilt (related to abandoning him), and fear of being totally unconnected to anyone, plus his compulsive need to succeed and poor self-image as a male. Most of their days were marked by unvoiced anger, withdrawal, and depression. Mr. Z., successful in other areas of his life, felt a failure in the marriage. Mrs. Z., who had always felt unattractive and unintelligent, was surprised and awed by her recent success as a commercial artist.

Abandonment was a central theme for Mrs. Z., as was her frequent, tearful declarations that she needed no one. Her father had died when she was a youngster. She perceived her mother as childlike, cold, and unloving, preferring a younger sister. Mr. Z. handled much of his anxiety by intellectualization. He placed all of the difficulties in the relationship on his wife, excusing her because of her unhappy childhood. Although miserable, he repeatedly stated he could not contemplate giving up on the marriage, as this would spell failure. His father had drummed into him that, above all, to be a good person he had always to do his utmost to succeed, and success meant being "the best." His mother gave support to this requirement by the quiet expression of terrible hurt and disappointment whenever he faltered. Thus he always worked harder than his colleagues, assuring himself he was the best.

The Z marriage had been pseudo-stable for many years and seemed to have been thrown off balance to some extent by the husband's growing sense of aging, but, more significantly, by the wife's individual developmental change. Her successful career and fuller self-responsibility resulted in increased feelings of adequacy with consequent diminution of appreciation of her husband. She withdrew from him with greater frequency and he responded by more desperate attempts "to support her and make her strong." Failing response, he, too, would withdraw and brood.

Mr. Z. rarely stated his desires, declaring that true caring was demonstrated by the ability to anticipate and intuitively know the other's wants. Mrs. Z., believing she would not be heard, also rarely expressed her wants directly—only what she did not want. Open, direct expression of anger was completely unacceptable to both. Mrs. Z. seemed never in her life to have given herself this right, and Mr. Z. interpreted such an expression as total rejection—as a write-off of relationship.

The couple's transactions showed little in the way of positive mutuality. They had different interests, and different friends, and often went separate ways. Mrs. Z. frequently refused social contact with her husband's professional associates and maintained distance from her own. For the most part she engaged in solitary pursuits.

One of the initial focal areas of therapy had to be support of Mrs. Z.'s tentative but growing awareness of herself as a competent person and her expression of this within the contexts of both the marital and therapeutic relationships. Correspondingly, the husband's tolerance of this growth had to be nurtured. Thus another initial focal target area was Mr. Z.'s excessive and compulsive requirement that he always be "the best." For him to become less driven and to be able to relinquish, even minimally, the parental role and to feel less threat from his wife's development, his own strict self-requirement had to be gradually lessened. It was necessary to help him incorporate the notion that in doing his best he was not always doing the best for others. There also had to be attention to his poor image of himself as a desirable male, which contributed to his overdoing for his wife and to his fear of loss of her dependency. Bearing in mind the couple's dynamics and the focal target areas, the initial modality(ies) and the techniques through which the target areas might be effected had to be chosen.

Modalities

Modality is both context and tool of therapy. The modality alternatives are one to one, conjoint (family or couple), and groups (nonkinship and couple). Initial use of one modality may enable later use of another when there is increased trust in the therapist or enhanced self-image. A shift in modality and technique may also be indicated with shift in focal target areas or client goals. There also may be combined use of modalities for different purposes.

It must be borne in mind that the marital couple is an ongoing part of the therapeutic system that usually continues in interaction outside of the therapy hour. The positive side of this is that the couple has the opportunity to continue work outside a conjoint session on issues addressed in the session. A noxious issue is that consequences of conjoint therapeutic sessions may be physical or emotional punishment of one partner by the other. Consequently, the "victim" partner may "walk on eggs" in the presence of the mate. In other situations, deep feelings of insecurity may act to constrict one or both partners.

Marital partners usually have a history of interaction with each other, and have subtle means of communication of which not only the therapist but they, themselves, may be consciously unaware. Thus the therapist who sees the couple only conjointly may not recognize distorted content resulting from inhibiting signals sent to block exposure.

A therapist who is of the same gender as the spouse automatically might be perceived as an ally of the spouse by virtue of gender. Common demonstrations of this perception are the statements, "All men (or women) are the same" and "All women (or men) stick together." In such a situation an initial use of conjoint sessions as the primary modality would more likely than not result in the "disadvantaged" spouse's early withdrawal from counseling unless he or she were very highly motivated and/or anxious about the consequences of such withdrawal. Use of a female–male team with the couple, if there were no other contraindications for the conjoint modality, might serve to eliminate the problem, and also might help to break the transference stereotype.

A therapist who is of a different gender than the spouse, by virtue of gender, also might be perceived as a rival for the spouse, depending on client self-image and the nature of defenses and transference. In this situation separate therapists of like sex well might be indicated for each partner.

In conjoint or family unit therapy, countertransference is more likely to be elicited than in one-to-one or unrelated groups. In multiperson sessions a single therapist can have difficulty in encompassing the multiple concurrent interactions expressed nonverbally as well as verbally. In any modality content may be distorted, mindfully or otherwise, in an effort to gain the therapist as ally.

If the foregoing factors do not contraindicate, conjoint therapy may be an appropriate ongoing modality of choice when both individuals are motivated to focus on enhancement of the relationship rather than on own personal problems, provided that there are no significant secrets that are a barrier to mutual openness in therapy. Additionally, this modality may be used to work through issues of separation. It is necessary that the same techniques be helpful to both partners, that neither partner makes predominant use of defenses of distortion and projection, and that cultural norms of partners are not violated.

An exception to these conditions may have to be made when one or both mates initially cannot tolerate separate individual sessions. Conjoint sessions may be needed to attempt to establish trust.

A couples' group may be appropriate as an adjunct to the conjoint modality when a multiplicity of role models and of transference objects is desirable and an arena is needed for deepening of self-awareness, reality testing, and experimentation with new behavior.

The same objectives may be met more properly in nonkinship mixed male and female groups for either or both partners when marital goals are disparate or when individual issues and/or individuation have become primary target areas. Lack of trust or fear of the partner also may be considerations pointing to use of a nonkinship group, providing there is trust of the therapist.

A family group may be the initial modality of choice with concurrent or subsequent separate work with the marital and other subsystems when marital conflict is focused on the children and the children seem to be symptomatically carrying or acting out the marital conflict. Additionally, it may be indicated when the family seems to be an undifferentiated ego mass with none or very fluid individual or marital couple boundaries. (In using this modality, parental roles must not be violated.)

A one-to-one modality is appropriate when individual concerns are the focal target areas or when marital goals are disparate and trust in the therapist is tenuous. It is also advisable when there is minimal ability to form a trusting relationship with others and/or there is frequent use of primitive defenses and/or the encouragement of dependency on the therapist is part of the therapeutic strategy.

Techniques

People suffering marital stress, as with any other kind of stress, can be assisted to substitute rewarding for dysfunctional behaviors and to free themselves from crippling anxieties, fears, and conflicts by a variety of techniques used creatively in varying combinations.

Generally an action-oriented approach is most successful with couples, as with individuals, in a high state of anxiety or crisis who literally do not know what to do. Action helps to bind the anxiety. When anxiety is not high, however, techniques such as explicitly suggested rehearsal of new behaviors will be resisted when negative transference and control are issues, or there is a reservoir of strong hostility. Whether the new behaviors relate to the couple's desire to effect changes in sexual behavior, or in less highly charged areas, resistance should be anticipated with these partners even in nongraded "no failure" innocuous exercises. In such instances insight and/or problem-solving techniques are initially more effective.

On the other hand, when authority and control are not issues and clients are each requesting behavior change for self, the action-oriented approach may be the most appropriate, possibly combined with techniques of an ego-supportive, problem-solving nature. Often insight follows action, and the therapist will sensitively follow the client's lead.

When dependency is the issue, techniques are called for that reach for feelings and the creation of a safe relationship for client insight and acceptance of dependency. The same is true in reference to sexual and aggressive feelings, the two great taboos of our culture.

When clients are oriented to introspection and transference seriously blocks or distorts their significant relationship, primary use of insight-oriented techniques may be necessary before action techniques can be used comfortably. In actuality it has been found that adherents of any one theoretical approach use a combination of techniques (Orten and Weis, 1974, Martin, 1975).

The Z. Case Continued. In the Z. situation, in consideration of the focal target areas, the nature of the couple's transactions with each other, and the rigidity of their defenses, primarily Mrs. Z.'s use of projection and withdrawal and Mr. Z.'s use of intellectualization, the therapist chose initially to work with them individually with planned evaluative conjoint conferences. Within a short time Mr. Z. agreed to join a group in which it was believed the role-modeling of others, especially a father figure, might help him ease his self-requirements.

About this time Mrs. Z. confided her secret. There was another man; she no longer was interested in her husband and wished to separate from him. The focus moved to her issues of abandonment and guilt tied to her parental relationships and her father's death, with primary use of insight-oriented techniques. Later, action techniques were used for rehearsal of how she might communicate her decision to her husband. Conjoint interviews were used to help resolve the couple's disparate goals for the marriage and to work through their separation. Mrs. Z. decided she had accomplished her goals and terminated treatment when she was settled in what she labeled as her "first own home." Mr. Z. remained in group, working through his failure and grief feelings. Gradually he stopped working so many extra hours in his employment and started taking brief holidays, sometimes with new women friends. He began to feel attractive to women and indicated satisfaction with his new life. However, direct expression of anger remained unacceptable to him.

Another Couple—Another Strategy

Mrs. D. requested a conjoint appointment for herself and her husband, defining the main difficulty as lack of communication. Both were outstandingly handsome and bright; they were in their late 20s. Mrs. D. verbalized with ease, had quick humor and an air of openness. Mr. D., on the other hand, was reticent in speaking and stuttered. He was extremely anxious about his wife's wish to work part-time and achieve some degree of independence. He felt such an action would be a critical threat to their marriage and had refused further discussion of the matter. Whenever Mrs. D. attempted to press disccussion, he withdrew into silence. When she finally "exploded," he withdrew even further. They had been locked in this conflict for almost two months.

The couple, married eight years, had known and enjoyed each other since childhood. From the time they were adolescents it had been taken for granted that they would marry. This they did after Mrs. D's college graduation and Mr. D's return from Vietnam, where he had served in a noncombat position. They had two children, a 7-year-old son and a 5-year-old daughter.

The D's agreed that their marriage had been a good one, although there had been some rough spots, particularly in the first two years. A year after their marriage and shortly after the birth of their son, Mr. D., an army officer, was stationed overseas for seven months. He felt that on his return his wife had a hard time "releasing the reins." When he was again assigned overseas, he urged his wife, newly pregnant, to come with their child. They enjoyed three years abroad. Both claimed that the premature birth and death of their second child drew them closer together. There was no difficulty with the birth of their daughter.

After leaving the service, Mr. D. managed a large family inheritance, maintaining his office at home where he also closely supervised all family expenditures. With both children in school, Mrs. D. expanded her volunteer activities and had recently been invited to work part-time in a friend's boutique.

Mrs. D. was eight years senior to her only sibling, a brother. Her parents were loving but "moralistic." It was mandatory to have only loving feelings toward family members because to have angry feeling was to be bad. Mr. D. was the third of five siblings. He had grown up feeling isolated within his family system. His mother had been hospitalized several times for mental illness during his childhood. She was prone to frequent violent outbursts, and often he was the butt of her verbal and physical abuse. He believed she had always hated him. He was sent to a boarding school when he was 12. He recalled intense conflict between his parents, usually escalating to physical battles. They divorced when he was 14. Although his siblings chose to remain with his mother, Mr. D. went with his father, described as a strict taskmaster who allowed his children only bare necessities.

The D.'s verbalized admiration and regard for each other, but the direct expression of anger was taboo for both. Whereas Mrs. D. could be direct in her expression of affection, this was a difficult area for Mr. D., who used sexual intimacy as the primary avenue for such expression. It also seemed to be used, almost compulsively, as a mode of feeling some connection. In their relationships with extended family, they often felt "pulled apart," trying to satisfy everyone. They had a variety of mutual interests and many friends, which Mr. D. attributed to his wife's charisma. He was troubled that he rarely participated actively in social discussions, believing that he had nothing of value to offer.

The therapist evaluated the marriage as having been stable. It had become shaky with the movement into parenthood. In addition, Mrs. D.'s ability to function independently during her husband's absence was felt by him as a loss of his control and a threat to the marriage. Some feelings of displacement by the baby may have rekindled old painful feelings of isolation and rejection. Restabilization of the marriage had been effected through a speedy return to a close symbiotic-like living situation, with minimal involvement outside of the nuclear family system. Mrs. D.'s later thrust toward increased individuation, related to the growth of the children and the changed maternal role, was perceived by Mr. D. as his wife's wanting to leave home. It also coincided with stressful role changes experienced by him in the transition from a nondemanding life as an army officer to civilian responsibilities.

Both partners were highly motivated to attain their shared goal —restabilization of the marriage. The immediate focal target had to be amelioration of Mr. D.'s panic linked to the old unhappy childhood feelings that had been triggered. He needed help in separating the present from the past and regaining some sense of control. A related target was the couple's dysfunctional pattern of communication in coping with disagreement and anger; both needed help toward neutralization of anger taboos tied to their parental introjections. In addition, it was necessary to address Mrs. D.'s conviction that she was evil when she attended to her own desires and did not hold herself in a subservient role to others, and Mr. D.'s meager self-esteem demonstrated by his belief that his only value lay in his fortune.

Mr. and Mrs. D. quickly formed a therapeutic alliance. The mutuality of their goals, the nature of the target areas, and the absence of negative transference and primitive defenses were additional criteria pointing to initial use of the conjoint modality. This also supported symbolically the continuing marital relatedness.

They were helped to express "dangerous" thoughts and feelings directly. Eventually each chose to work on individual problems, and later each entered separate, small nonkinship therapy groups. Thus personal internalized difficulties became an individual responsibility instead of being played out in the marital context. Mrs. D. eventually was able to relate in a more open fashion with others. Mr. D. lost his stutter and began to recognize his self-worth.

CONCLUSIONS

There has been explication of essential content in the study-assessment and engagement phase in work with couples in stress. Determination of the relationship disequilibrators, marital status, and nature of each individual's motivation in the therapeutic venture has been shown as crucial in identifying the focal target areas and in setting realistic therapeutic goals. It is from consideration of these factors, along with knowledge of the individual and couple systems' functioning, and the quality of client–therapist relationships, that therapeutic strategy evolves.

As illustrated in the case material, different kinds of marriages and people with different reasons for requesting help require treatment tailored to their unique needs. Just as no one therapeutic strategy could possibly fit all client situations, so, too, it is doubtful that the same strategy in all of its parts could continue to be the most helpful throughout all phases of any therapeutic endeavor. Ongoing evaluation is essential to keep current with clients in flux. Thus the alertness, sensitivity, and creativity of the therapist are probably the most important factors of all in the shaping and reshaping of the therapeutic strategy in each situation.

REFERENCES

Ackerman, N. *Treating the Troubled Family*. New York: Basic Books, 1967.

Beck, D. F., and Jones, M. A. *Progress on Family Problems*. New York: Family Service Association of America, 1973.

Blanck, R., and Blanck, G. *Marriage and Personal Development*. New York: Columbia University Press, 1968.

Boszormenyi-Nagy, I., and Framo, J. (Eds.) *Intensive Family Therapy*. New York: Harper and Row, 1969.

Gurman, A. S. The Effects and Effectiveness of Marital Therapy. In Allen S. Gurman and David G. Rice (Eds.) *Couples in Conflict*. New York: Jason Aronson, 1975.

Haley, J. Family Therapy. *International Journal of Psychiatry*, 1970–1971, 9, 233–242.

Kempler, W. *Transcript of Conference Conducted at Family Institute*. Cardiff, Wales: Barnardo's Publications, 1975.

Lederer, W. J., and Jackson, D. D. *The Mirages of Marriage*. New York, W. W. Norton and Co., 1968.

Markowitz, M., and Kadis, A. L. Short-Term Analytic Treatment of Married Couples in a Group by a Therapist Couple. In B. F. Riess (Eds.) *New Directions in Mental Health*, Vol. 1. New York: Grune & Stratton, 1968.

Martin, P. A. *A Marital Therapy Manual*. New York: Brunner/Mazel, 1976.

Orton, J., and Weis, G. Strategies and Techniques for Therapeutic Change. *Social Service Review*. 1974, 48, 355–366.

Satir, V. *Conjoint Family Therapy*. Palo Alto, Calif.; Science and Behavior Books, 1967.

Walrond-Skinner, S. *Family Therapy*. Boston: Routledge and Kegan Paul, 1977.

CHERYL GROPPER AND
JANICE ZOLMAN BOGNER

8

Criminal Offenders: The Dilemma of Involuntary Treatment

ONE GENERALLY ACCEPTED precondition of therapy is that the client be sufficiently motivated for the task—that is, enough anxiety and pain have accumulated to cause a conscious wish for help. Without this motivation, the client is viewed as unready for psychotherapy. When clients enter a treatment relationship, they generally are able to verbalize that a problem is causing them pain and that they have a desire to solve problems through psychotherapy. Involuntary clients often lack this motivation, but this lack should not be used as an excuse not to treat them; it is possible to engage the unmotivated client, as illustrated through clinical work with criminal offenders.

THE PUSHED-AHEAD CLIENT

Argelander (1976) refers to clients who lack the stress of suffering and readiness for treatment as "sent-on-ahead" or "pushed-ahead" clients: "He comes not on his own initiative, but under pressure from another person—a parent [or] spouse...other people are more interested in [the patient's] treatment than is the patient himself." (p. 43)

According to Perlman (1978) and Temperley (1979), a significant percentage of social work clients in the United States and Great Britain indeed resist social work intervention. In private or voluntary public settings clinical social workers commonly receive referrals of resistant or unmotivated clients. The profession has been called on in a variety of ways to evaluate, diagnose, and treat clients who are "pushed ahead," unmotivated, or involuntary. For example, when a child is referred as the identified client by the school or court system, the worker may find that the parents are not ready to accept help for themselves or the child, despite the child's serious problems (Feldman, 1958). It is not unusual to have as resistive clients abusive parents who deny any problems or clients with psychosomatic symptoms who are convinced their problems are medical. One or more members of family or marital units are often in treatment involuntarily. The involuntary nature of treatment becomes even more poignant when referral for treatment is stipulated by the court.

MOTIVATION

The "unmotivated patient syndrome" described by Nir and Cutler (1978) applies to clients such as alcoholics, offenders, and members of lower socioeconomic groups, who seem reluctant to accept treatment and are unwilling to cooperate. In addition to intrapsychic factors, cognitive styles, cultural biases, and beliefs contribute to this reluctance. As Holt asked in 1967, how can we expect all clients to be able to want help and be knowledgeable enough about psychotherapy to request it? "For some, and to some extent for all to have to be helped involves an unconsciously expected repetition of earlier humiliations and anxiety about being weak. [Motivation is] inseparable from the patient's infantile needs, conflicts and defenses" (p. 1319). Some clients have greater ego motivation to recognize distress, but the conscious ego decision regarding treatment has unconscious derivatives, and it is the balance of these two factors that mobilizes a person to engage in treatment. Thus the important question is not whether there is "good" or "bad" motivation for treatment; the emphasis should be on understanding how conscious and unconcious factors determine motivation and how these factors affect the person who accepts and begins treatment.

Resistance that appears during ongoing therapy is usually expected and accepted. As Eidelberg (1968) defined it, resistance is "the power responsible for...keeping the repressed content from becoming conscious..." (p. 377). According to Greenson (1967), it is "in essence to counterforce in the patient, operating against the process of analysis, the analyst, and the analytic procedures and processes..." (p. 60). Indeed, Freud (1913) remarked that an individual's attitude toward treatment is unimportant because resistance arises as soon as that individual is under study. As Blanck and Blanck (1974) have pointed out, "Therapists tend to have far more tolerance for resistance in its unconscious forms than for resistance which has found conscious rationalization and is displaced upon beginning treatment" (p. 197).

To have a client reject help despite clinical evidence of conflict or social problems can be frustrating and ungratifying for therapists. Temperley (1979) points out that social workers strongly identify with clients and their suffering and hope to be viewed as enabling allies. Thus workers may not know how to cope with feelings of impotence or of being misused or exploited by a client's negative transference. Because they are more comfortable viewing themselves as experts who are available to those who want to benefit from professional knowledge and skills, it is not surprising that many avoid working with involuntary clients.

THE CRIMINAL OFFENDER

For the court, involuntary psychiatric treatment is an important option in the judicial sentencing process because it represents an attempt to give offenders an opportunity to learn to cope better with the problems that they may have "acted out" through the offense. While it can be argued that nonintrusive verbal psychotherapy by force represents an abuse of the client's right to refuse treatment, it can also be argued that, without forced treatment, many offenders would not have the chance to learn new ways of controlling their behavior. Kaplan et al. (1969), for example, pointed out that enforced treatment can help offenders to achieve greater ego control in place of being controlled externally by incarceration. As forced treatment becomes more widely used by the courts and as states institute legal statutes mandating psychiatric intervention, the number of offenders who come involuntarily to the attention of mental health practioners will increase.

Since referral for treatment is initiated by the court, clients often associate treatment with the judicial system. Consequently, establishing a therapeutic alliance between worker and client involves special problems. First, because the court has the authority to stipulate treatment despite a client's refusal, the client's ensuing hostility and resistance toward authority are often displaced on the therapists. Second, workers need to ally themselves with their clients; at the same time, however, they must accept the alliance with the court or probation department as a source of referrals and funding. Third, social, cultural, and psychological factors contribute to treatment difficulties.

A recent study of adult offenders at a midwestern forensic clinic (Green, 1979) involved a sample population that was 66 percent male and 34 percent female, with approximately 80 percent white and 20 percent black; the average age was 28.6. Half of the offenders in the sample were single, 21 percent were married, 24 percent were separated or divorced, and 5 percent were widowed. The average education was 10.8 years. Approximately 40 percent of the sample was unemployed, and 55 percent were employed in skilled or unskilled labor. More than half were diagnosed as having character or personality disorders. The remaining diagnoses ranged from psychotic to adjustment reactions (those diagnosed as psychotic were referred for inpatient treatment). Thus the typical client in the sample was a single, white employed male in his late 20s who had not graduated from high school.

Although many offenders enter treatment with a *conscious* unwillingness to participate, their behavior is often a veiled unconscious attempt to receive help or control. The therapist may recognize that clinical symptoms such as depression, injuries to self-esteem, and the like led to an offense, but the client may lack the motivation to understand these dynamics. It is possible, however, to engage these clients in treatment despite conscious reluctance.

EMPATHY

How does one work with the conscious, immediate obstacle—the client's opposition to treatment? One basic principle in social work is that one begins where the client is. But implementing this concept, simple as it sounds, requires great skill because the therapist must be empathic to the conscious material the client is presenting. In 1959 Kohut described empathy and introspection as tools for psychological observation. In elaborating on this use of empathy, Palombo (1979) states that only through introspective merging with another person's feeling states, while simultaneously maintaining cognitive awareness of the merger, can one begin to know what another feels. According to Ornstein and Ornstein (1977),

"The empathizer makes no judgment about what the other should feel, but solicits the expression of whatever he does feel and for brief periods experiences these feelings on his own...permitting a view in which the patient's anxieties and mode of defenses are recognized as unique for him." (p. 6)

This recognition of presenting affects and their functions can reduce the anxiety associated with these affects. Empathic interpretation, as a specific mode of intervention, allows the therapist to mirror or connect with clients' resistance. This form of intervention does not involve confrontation or the tearing down of defenses; it allows clients to maintain the defenses they need for psychic survival. And since their defenses are not attacked, their anxiety is reduced and they are thus more able to verbalize the affects they are experiencing. Through this feeling of being understood, a process of working through begins and the therapeutic bond between therapist and client is promoted.

Offenders who enter treatment against their will often experience it as an assault and arrive at the first session with a chip on their shoulder, daring the therapist to knock it off. In other words, the therapist becomes a target for their conscious anger, hostility, and sense of being treated unfairly.

Rather than ignore the essential affects, the therapist must view them as the most important material with which to develop a connection. Those who proceed with other issues are following their own agendas, which in effect leaves clients to contend with this "resistance" on their own and increases the communication gap. Comments such as "Since you are here, let's try to see how we can best use the time" are examples of efforts to begin treatment while recognizing to some degree the client's lack of motivation. Yet, the therapist is ignoring the client's affect, in terms of the specific meaning of "since you are here." The therapist should handle these initial conscious resistances as one would handle other resistances in ongoing treatment; that is, by empathically understanding them and helping the client to work through these feelings. In so doing the therapist can promote an atmosphere in which the client is able to talk about other troubling issues.

POTENTIAL INTERFERENCES

A variety of obstacles confront therapists as they begin treatment with involuntary clients, especially those referred by the court. Although this population suffers a range of pathology, characterological disorders are most frequent. Long-standing patterns of maladaptive behavior that cause little or no anxiety are often difficult to reverse. Thus treatment can often be difficult because these clients experience a minimal amount of conscious suffering (Jackel, 1963).

In addition, sociocultural factors may interfere with development of a therapeutic relationship. As Nir and Cutler (1978) remind us, difficulties can arise from differences in attitudes, goals, and styles of communication and cognition. When working with offenders from lower socioeconomic groups, it is important to recognize the social, cultural, and environmental factors that influence their motivation for treatment. Hollis (1965) warned that low-income clients are not a homogeneous group and should not be stereotyped. Differences in ethnic background, class, education, and region affect their "standards of behavior, aspirations, and perceptions of others and of self" (Hollis, 1972, p. 17). In addition, workers must be sensitive to the effects of deprivation, poor education, devaluation, and limited opportunities in a status-minded society: "Motivation and aspiration are often not absent; but disappointment after disappointment and frustration after frustration may have forced .... [such a client] to bury his hopes for himself" and "craving for liking, respect, and help...may lie beneath... [his] hostile couldn't-care-less, touch-me-not exterior (Hollis, 1965, p. 466).

Hellenbrand (1961) also pointed out that the involuntary client's initial response to treatment may vary considerably, depending on cultural patterning and value orientation. For example, the nature and degree of motivation may depend upon "whether or not the client, as a result of his cultural conditioning, believes that personal efforts can effect changes in his behavior and in his situation"

(p. 164), and whether treatment is viewed as a respectable way of making changes.

Offenders often view treatment as degrading and as a sign that one is both weak and crazy. In addition, they tend to value action over verbal communication, to distrust authority figures, and to be present—rather than future—oriented. For many, crime is a way of life in the family and community. The treatment situation with offenders who come to treatment involuntarily involves a close interaction between intrapsychic and sociocultural forces; both must be recognized and assessed for the therapist to obtain a comprehensive understanding upon which therapeutic work can be based. Hollis (1972) said, "The worker must steer carefully between these twin errors, neither introducing culturally foreign goals because of personal preference for them nor feeling inhibited from trying to motivate the client to changes in culturally conditioned ways of behaving when his social functioning and personal well-being will be improved by such changes" (p. 290).

The therapist's responsibility to report the client's attendance to the court represents one serious obstacle to establishing a working relationship. Clients naturally associate the therapist with the court; as a result, fear of being reported to the court inhibits the free expression that is essential for therapy. The therapist must clearly delineate to clients what is and what is not reported to the court. Only by maintaining confidentiality about all information other than attendance can the therapist reduce the client's distrust.

It is important to realize that probation officers do not always use their authority to enforce attendance at treatment sessions. Often, their case loads are so large that they are unable to follow up on all clients referred for treatment. Some do not view therapy as rehabilitative, and this may influence their support of a client's attendance. In addition, violation of probation means that the client may be incarcerated; some probation officers view this as extreme punishment for missing treatment sessions. Therefore, whether the court's orders will be enforced depends on the discretion of the individual probation officer. Consequently, the therapist should develop a supportive relationship with the probation officer concerning treatment. This relationship can be fostered in several ways. The therapist can demonstrate a willingness to explain the general principles of treatment to probation officers so that they understand possible benefits as well as realistic limitations of treatment. Because probation officers are responsible for exerting external control over their clients by setting limits, they, like therapists, often become the receptacle for a client's anger. The therapist should recognize and express appreciation of the probation officer's difficult role. Regular informal and formal contact between the two concerning the differences and similarities in their respective roles helps to build alliances and prevent breakdowns in communication.

COUNTERTRANSFERENCE

Other issues that need to be addressed by the clinician include countertransference and the therapist's values and support systems. Working with involuntary clients, particularly those with character disorders, evokes significant countertransference issues. Often therapists do not like being discounted and rejected by clients. It is even more difficult to be the recipient of anger from clients who do not feel they have problems and thus do not want treatment. Even if an alliance is established and treatment is effective, many of these clients cannot verbalize that they have been helped; therefore, the therapist must look for other indicators of effectiveness, such as the client's attendance, increased introspection, better coping skills, and improved interpersonal relationships. Temperley (1979) states that:

The most damaged among social work clients have inner worlds that are bound to be dominated by persecuting and attacking figures, and we hesitate to take positions where we sense we are likely to be seen in terms of these figures....we are afraid of being seen and even seeing ourselves as damaging and bad and hated figures (pp. 5–6).

Therapists who have strong needs to be liked and overtly appreciated by their clients can be hurt and offended by a client who is hostile or who does not want help. According to Spotnitz (1969, p. 172), the therapist who is wounded by these kinds of reactions "tends to get lost in narcissistic preoccupations and doubts" and may actually hope the client does not come back. The therapist who does not rely on positive feedback from clients can explore their overt resistance to treatment without becoming defensive or overwhelmed by feelings of inadequacy, hurt, and anger.

Therapists working with criminal offenders also must be aware of their own value systems. An attitude of interest and acceptance is essential during any treatment process, but this attitude may be difficult to maintain if the client has assaulted someone or stolen or destroyed property. It may be even more difficult if the client purposefully committed the crime and expresses little or no guilt about the action. However, interest and acceptance do not mean condoning actions that are destructive and illegal: "Acceptance means that whether the worker approves or disapproves of what the client has told about himself, he continues to feel and convey a positive, understanding attitude toward the client" (Hollis, 1972, p. 91). In other words, the therapist must be able to step back from judging the client's actions and try to understand what function these actions serve.

Because the therapist's gratifications are neither obvious nor immediate, it is important to build in solid support systems to help with this difficult but challenging treatment situation. These support systems can range from formal supervision to informal contact with colleagues. Without a support system, the therapist is likely to feel depleted, which can interfere with the treatment process.

CASE STUDIES

Once an alliance has been established, treatment of offenders is similar to treatment of voluntary clients, varying with the client need and disturbance. The following clinical examples illustrate how the therapist can share with the client an empathic understanding of the latter's conscious resistance to treatment.

Mrs. Y., a 55-year-old white, married woman employed as a bookkeeper, was referred by the court for treatment after she was convicted of shoplifting items valued at more than $150. Mrs. Y. came to the first session feeling extremely humiliated, ashamed, and embarrassed, and perceived treatment as a punishment for her crime. Although she felt she deserved to be punished, she did not believe she needed treatment. When the therapist expressed her appreciation of how painful it was for Mrs. Y. to come to treatment sessions because it was a constant reminder of her misdeed, Mrs. Y. was able to verbalize further and become aware of her perception of herself as bad, not only in relation to her offense, but in general.

Because the therapist responded empathically to her initial resistance to treatment, Mrs. Y. was able to work through this resistance and examine the specific dynamics of her offense. As an alliance began to develop, the therapist focused on helping Mrs. Y. understand the function her shoplifting had served. From an early age, Mrs. Y. had felt a deep sense of deprivation and an overwhelming need for restitution because of it. For years she had wondered, "When is it going to be my turn? When will someone give to me?" When her father needed care and expressed a desire to move in with her, her early struggles and conflicts over dependency were reawakened and she experienced such feelings of deprivation that her strong sense of right and wrong was overwhelmed and she was able to shoplift. The department store had provided Mrs. Y. with a convenient way of giving to herself by making items easily accessible.

Mr. P., age 20, a single, white man with a previous record, was referred to the clinic after a charge of assaulting a policeman. An anxious, inhibited young man with few close relationships, Mr. P. clearly viewed treatment as "getting the shaft," especially since he had already received a jail sentence, a fine, and a period of probation. In the beginning the therapist shared with Mr. P. her appreciation of his feeling that treatment was another punishment he did not deserve. This allowed him to discuss his feelings about treatment openly. Although he remained bitter about treatment throughout, he attended the sessions regularly. Because he was allowed to maintain his anger about treatment, he was able to preserve his self-esteem and begin thinking about the behavior that had brought him into conflict with the police. The material that emerged led both therapist and client to realize that all his arrests over the past three years had occurred in August, the month in which he had first been arrested, and seemed to be attempts to master the guilt and shame related to the first arrest. This cognitive understanding of his behavior led Mr. P. to feel a greater sense of control over his actions.

Mr. L. was a 32-year-old white, divorced, employed man who had been convicted of breaking and entering and was referred for treatment as a stipulation of his probation. During the first session Mr. L. clearly indicated that he did not need treatment because his life was going well; he planned to remarry and looked to his fiancee for any needed support. He announced that he would not tell the therapist anything because it was his business and she could not alter his thinking. The therapist expressed her appreciation of how unfair having to come to the clinic must seem to Mr. L. Mr. L. responded by saying how unjust it was to make a man of his standing appear in court, pay a fine, and submit to treatment. Thus the therapist, by recognizing Mr. L.'s need for control and his anger over the loss of it as well as the narcissistic injury of becoming a client, connected with Mr. L.'s resistance and allowed him to feel understood. Consequently, he was able to talk more comfortably about his feelings. As his anxiety was reduced, his posture became more natural and his thoughts more spontaneous.

During four months of treatment, the therapist and Mr. L. were able to focus on understanding the dynamics involved in his arrest. He came to acknowledge the intensity of his responses to perceived rejection from others; the specific act of breaking and entering seemed to be one of retaliation. After an argument with his boss about his work, which Mr. L. viewed as an attack on his self-esteem, he had broken into his employer's place of business while under the influence of alcohol. Although Mr. L. talked as if he had achieved an understanding of his behavior, one could not be sure that this was integrated emotionally.

It is important to remember that these clients came to treatment involuntarily at the court's direction, and in all cases a specified period of treatment was mandated. However, in many situations this order is not obeyed, and frequently it is not enforced by the court or the probation department. Because the therapist in each case empathized with the initial conscious resistance to treatment and understood the unconscious resistance, the clients were able to stay in treatment for the required period; they were not pushed away. During this time there was a beginning examination of the specific dynamics of their offenses. It is not common for clients to choose to extend their treatment after the period mandated by the court, although some do. Some choose to continue treatment in other facilities because of the stigma attached to this beginning period; others do not continue anywhere. However, if this contact were benign and less threatening than originally expected, one might hope that the potential for help within a therapeutic relationship would be remembered and chosen as a resource at another time.

CONCLUSIONS

Working with the criminal offender who comes to treatment involuntarily is a difficult but challenging process. By being aware of and sensitized to the subtle elements upon which the formation of *any* treatment relationship is predicated, and by developing the techniques required to work with conscious resistance, the therapist is better able to reach clients who seem unreachable.

Motivation for treatment is a frequently used but unclear concept. By utilizing conscious motivation as a criterion for treatability, clinicians run the risk of overlooking a significant group of clients who need and might benefit from therapy. True, some involuntary clients do not respond to any kind of therapeutic intervention. But perhaps the knowledge and skill required to understand and engage these clients are not yet available to the clinicians who work with them.

REFERENCES

Argelander, H. *The Initial Interview in Psychotherapy*, New York: Human Sciences Press, 1976.

Blanck, G., and Blanck, R. *Ego Psychology Theory and Practice*. New York: Columbia University Press, 1974.

Eidelberg, L. *Encyclopedia of Psychoanalysis*. New York: Free Press, 1968.

Feldman, Y. A Casework Approach Toward Understanding Parents of Emotionally Disturbed Children. *Social Work*, July 1958 3, 23–29.

Freud, S. On Beginning Treatment (Further Recommendations on the Technique of Psycho-analysis). J. Strachey (Ed.) *The Standard Edition of the Complete Psychological Works of Sigmund Freud, Vol. 12 (1911–1913)*. London: Hogarth Press, 1975.

Green, B.L. Court Psychiatric Center Treatment Program Assessment. Unpublished manuscript, University of Cincinnati, Department of Psychiatry, 1979.

Greenson, R.R. *The Technique and Practice of Psychoanalysis*. New York: International Universities Press, 1967.

Hellenbrand, S.C. Client Value Orientations: Implications for Diagnosis and Treatment. *Social Casework*, April 1961, 42, 163–169.

Hollis, F. *Casework: A Psychosocial Therapy*. New York: Random House, 1972.

Hillis, F. Casework and Social Class. *Social Casework*, October 1965, 46, 463–471.

Holt, W. The Concept of Motivation for Treatment. *American Journal of Psychiatry*, May 1967, 123, 1388–1394.

Jackel, M.M. Clients with Character Disorders. *Social Casework*, June 1963, 44, 315–322.

Kaplan, M., et al. The Control or Acting-Out in the Psychotherapy of Delinquents. In S.A. Szurek and I.N. Berlin (Eds.) The Antisocial Child: His Family and His Community. *Langley Porter Child Psychiatry Series, Vol. 4*. Palo Alto, Calif.: Science and Behavior Books, 1969.

Kohut, H. Introspection, Empathy, and Psychoanalysis. *Journal of American Psychoanalytic Association*, 1959, 7, 459–483.

Nir, Y., and Cutler, R. The Unmotivated Patient Syndrome: Survey of Therapeutic Interventions. *American Journal of Psychiatry*, 1978, 135, 442–447.

Ornstein, A., and Ornstein, P. The Nature of Interpretations in Psychoanalytic Psychotherapy. Unpublished manuscript, University of Cincinnati, Department of Psychiatry, 1977.

Palombo, J. The Psychoanalytic Psychology of The Self: An Overview. Unpublished manuscript, Chicago Institute for Psychoanalysis, 1979.

Perlman, H.H. Relationships. Paper presented at the meeting of the Ohio Chapter of the National Association of Social Workers, Ohio Chapter of the Social Service Association, and Ohio Society for Clinical Social Work, Cincinnati, Ohio, November 1978.

Spotnitz, H. *Modern Psychoanalysis of the Schizophrenic Patient*. New York: Grune & Stratton, 1969.

Temperley, J. The Implications for Social Work Practice of Recent Psychoanalytic Developments. In *Change and Renewal in Psychodynamic Social Work British and American Developments in Practice and Education for Services to Families and Children. Proceedings of the Oxford Conference*, England, 1979.

Part Three
ADOLESCENTS AND CHILDREN

FLORENCE LIEBERMAN

9

The Mixed-Age Group as an Adolescent's Transitional Family

BECAUSE ADOLESCENTS NEED the stimulus and support of peers for healthy development, a variety of group activities with others of a similar age commonly flourish at this time of life. Thus participation in a therapeutic group with other adolescents has frequently been helpful to the young person who is isolated, different, or distrustful of adults (Berkowitz and Sugar, 1975).

Yet enthusiasm for this modality has at times resulted in its indiscriminate and even dangerous use. For example, a combination of encounter and confrontation techniques and leadership by untrained youths has subjected some young people to dangerous psychological assault (Lieberman, Caroff, and Gottesfeld, 1973). Often the focus of these groups has been adaptive behavior and feeling better in the present rather than self-sustaining, long-term changes in personality (Spotnitz, 1971).

Some adolescents, especially those with severe problems and fears, are not ready for peer groups because they are unable to risk themselves in this way. Their primary need is for intensive, devel-

---

This chapter is a revised version of a paper delivered at the annual meeting of the American Orthopsychiatric Association, Washington, D. C., April 1979.

opmentally oriented, long-term treatment. Within this framework, a therapeutic group composed of members of varying ages and diagnoses may stimulate therapeutic work, and provide support that will enable extremely troubled youngsters to work on age-appropriate tasks. Because it mirrors the disparate ages within a natural family, a heterogeneous group can serve as an alternative, transitional family for some disturbed adolescents who reflect and have internalized their family's pathology.

ADOLESCENT TASKS AND PEER GROUPS

Adolescence is one stage in a series of developmental stages, each associated with age-specific psychosocial tasks (Erikson, 1963; Freud, 1905). The tasks of adolescence have been conceptualized as changes in attitudes to the physical body, to oedipal objects, and to contemporaries (Laufer, 1977), completion of a second-individuation phase (Blos, 1967), and reformulation of identity (Erikson, 1956). Adolescents need to give up what is known and predictable and work toward an indefinite future.

Physical maturation can occur without concomitant psychological development—obviously physical development does not automatically result in psychological maturity. But for all adolescents, maturation of the body and its primary and secondary sex organs and the increase in sexual and aggressive drives upset any equilibrium attained in childhood. In addition, others in the young person's social environment tend to react and interact differently, expressing new expectations for current and future behaviors. Therefore, psychological changes are inevitable. Normally, the complex interplay of inner and outer forces, modified by new knowledge, experiences, and abilities, leads to changes in functioning.

The crucial task—achievement of individual identity; a sense of being one's own self in one's own body in one's own particular society—usually is not completed until the end of adolescence (Davidson, 1974) because old identifications with parents are not modified until new identifications are available. Blos (1967) compares the second individuation phase of adolescence to infancy, when there is a hatching to become an individuated toddler; in adolescence the shedding of family dependencies is again accompanied by intrapsychic changes.

During normal adolescent struggles and ambivalence related to dependence and independence, peers provide support. Increased relations with peers often begin as a negative flight from the family and progress toward positive acceptance of peers as realistic and dependable sources of emotional sustenance (Meeks, 1974). The adolescent peer group can function as a transitional object that enables and supports psychological separation from the familiar parental environment. Although many spontaneously formed peer groups resemble the family situation, adolescents usually find them easier to cope with because obedience to group rules is voluntary. Furthermore, it is possible to become the leader of the group—a possibility that does not exist in most natural families (Buxbaum, 1970).

The peer group permits its members to try out roles without permanent commitment, enables experimentation with severing oneself from childhood dependencies, widens the experiential field, and provides opportunities for new identifications (Blos, 1976). It can also aid in the transition from the dependence of childhood to the independence of adulthood.

ADOLESCENT DISTURBANCE

Groups and peers can become new dependencies for adolescents who have not developed the capacity to use either their social environment or their peer groups progressively. In complying with the group and its code, some may abandon the parental value system for that of others and remain alienated and undefined. Others, unable to tolerate the painful and confusing disengagement from parents, may withdraw from their peers (Meeks, 1974).

Disturbance in adolescence may represent a continuation of previous difficulties, an amplification of overlooked problems, or a completely new set of problems. Some teenagers seem to regress; others remain children, not changing at all. Some seriously disturbed youths who seemed to be treated successfully in latency have a recurrence of early pathology. Although the earlier therapy provided emotional support, the need to disengage from the family in adolescence may cause regression and necessitate more treatment. Developmentally oriented treatment of the adolescent will focus on enabling the strength to take the chance to engage in age-appropriate tasks. Often this necessitates intensive individual treatment to establish trust and the ability to turn to the therapist for new identifications. The dilemma is that this may too easily become a transfer of dependency from parents to therapist.

Concurrent group and individual treatments can dilute, modify, and divide the transference by providing multiple models. Identification, a major dynamic in group psychotherapy, is automatic and largely unconscious. Slavson (1964) suggests this can be therapeutic if it neutralizes or corrects undesirable ego functioning and defenses and replaces faulty identifications through the use of verbal catharsis and discharge of noxious memories and feelings.

THE MIXED-AGE GROUP

It is generally accepted that age spans must be small in groups conducted for children, adolescents, or the elderly (Spotnitz, 1971). Most groups should be planned around homogeneity of interests and age and heterogeneity of personalities. Wide age differences may stimulate displacement and reactions of a parent–child type with basic transferences becoming as negative as are feelings toward real parents (Slavson, 1964).

On the other hand, basic group themes tend to revolve around sexual problems and emotional discontent with parents and siblings. These are areas of great concern to most adolescents. Though adults may have had more experiences than the adolescent and usually have made more significant life-changing decisions, these often have occurred with little knowledge or understanding. Even though adults are older, some may be struggling with unresolved problems not unlike those with which the adolescent is concerned. Then their therapeutic tasks may not be so different.

Although group psychotherapy focuses on feelings, communication is through language and concepts. Therefore intellectual compatibility is of great importance. Many adolescents do have the capacity to think and speak as well as most adults. Individuals of disparate ages can be grouped together if they have similar intellectual capacities and are willing and able to accept a working alliance.

Glatzer (1978) considers the working alliance to be the healthy potential of therapy groups. Stimulated by the group process, this alliance is the realistic collaboration between clients and therapist and among clients. It is different from unconscious, unrealistic transferences. It can assist in motivating those with fragile ego resources as well as safeguard against the leader's mistakes and countertransferences. Thus the group and the therapist help each other to support the appropriate defenses of individual members and to work for self-sustained change.

The following case histories illustrate how an adolescent boy and a 50-year-old man were able to use the same group therapeutically.

JASON

Jason B., age 16½, had been treated during latency at a child guidance clinic for underachievement, isolation, and fears. Jason was his parents' symptom: all their complaints centered on him although they had severe individual and marital problems of their own. Jason's early treatment prevented a serious breakdown, enabled some growth, and, as Jason once put it, "It was a restful, quiet place to come to when home was all confused."

Over 6 feet tall, broad shouldered, dark haired, and able to grow a heavy mustache or beard at will, Jason was still a baby and felt like one. He had a petulant manner, exhibited an infantile dependency on his parents, and had internalized their depression and low expectations. Although he complained that his parents picked on him, he stayed close to home, depended on his parents for his social life, and traveled alone only to school and back. Despite his size, he perceived himself as the small, fat boy he had once been. He was interested in clothes, but dressed as his father did, borrowing Mr. B's clothing, particularly his underwear and socks. Thus Jason looked peculiar because he dressed like an older man. His language was faultless, his vocabulary rich, sophisticated, and studded with humor, metaphors, and sarcasm—he spoke exactly as his father did.

Mr. and Mrs. B. complained about Jason's obstinacy, his messy room, and his failure to help with household chores; he was a failure in school as well because he did not work there. They also complained about each other and fought incessantly at home and in the therapist's office. Both struggled with obesity and depression. Mrs. B. somatized; Mr. B. spent his nonworking hours in bed. To them, everything was good or bad, Jason's blue-eyed, blonde sister represented the good part of them. Only 1½ years older than Jason, she did well in school, had friends, and married immediately after graduating from college. While her room was private, Jason's was the family garbage dump. For instance, because Jason's room had the largest closet, Mr. B. used it to store huge quantities of clothing, appliances, books, and magazines, none of which he ever discarded.

He went into Jason's room constantly to retrieve his possessions, and Mrs. B. went in to clean it up. Jason had no privacy.

Unlike most 16-year-olds, Jason thought it would be a good idea for the therapist to talk with his parents; then she would understand what he was up against. He still believed that his parents were omnipotent and, if they wished, could make everything better for him. He transferred this omnipotence to the therapist, who could make everything better for him by making his parents help him more. In other words, he wished them to change; he saw no reason to change himself.

Mr. and Mrs. B. wanted Jason to change. Whenever the therapist saw them with Jason, they began the session by yelling at and about him, they fought with each other. Mrs. B. resented her husband's pessismism and lack of sociability. Mr. B.—an angry, paranoid man—raged about minority groups, particularly blacks, whom he held responsible for all violence and crime in the world, and for his lack of progress on the job. Both parents believed in authority; they never doubted doctors, lawyers, teachers, and therapists, although they complained about how little Jason had improved. The therapist easily obtained their cooperation in relation to Jason's treatment by acknowledging the legitimacy of their concern, and relieving them of responsibility for managing what they viewed as their Frankenstein's monster.

Although he wore his father's clothing, Jason described himself as smaller than his father. "The mind," he said, "is one thing and the body another." Yet he somatized when anxious and had a phobic fear of injections and other medical and dental procedures. He defended against sexual preoccupations, masturbation, and fear of homosexuality by somatizing, and against feelings by joking. When the therapist listened carefully and communicated to his real feeling and meaning, Jason complained that she took everything he said seriously. She agreed, but said she was serious about helping him. He was aware that he joked when nervous, but he felt that people usually did not understand him and he liked being understood.

There were many ghosts in his life and many angry feelings. He was the only boy in the world who had been in the Girl Scouts—his mother had been den leader for his sister's group and he had attended the camp at which she worked. Jason spoke repeatedly of his anger and discomfort with these experiences. He was afraid of women, whom he regarded as controlling. Although he wished to identify with men, particularly his father, he was afraid of their aggression and his own and was equally afraid of loving feelings. When asked how he felt about seeing a woman therapist, Jason said she was a neuter: She was supposed to be.

Mr. B. would not permit "Sibling rivalry" (fighting) . Jason translated this into not competing, avoiding all activities where differences or conflict might occur or where he might be better than his sister, denigrating the value of achievement. Negatively different from his sister and everyone else, he learned to get attention by passivity.

He complained that the therapist was not assertive enough because she didn't tell him what to do; then he complained that she pushed him. When she pointed out his ambivalence, he was puzzled, remarking that if he wanted something, his parents would usually get it for him, even before he told them what he wanted. He never let anyone know what he wanted. At the moment he had only one good pair of shoes, but eventually this would bother his parents, who would buy him another pair. The therapist explained that this was how he got clothing suitable for an older man.

Jason was intellectually intrigued by the idea that mind and body were related and talked about his sexual feelings and his lack of knowledge. When he reached the age of 17, he thought he was as tall as his father; at 18 he said he was bigger than his father.

Isolation and struggle over achievement continued, even when Jason entered a community college near his home. He learned to use drugs, and after he had talked about drugs for several sessions, the therapist called this to his attention. Jason grinned and said he was asking her to help him stop taking drugs. He soberly noted that the campus reeked of them and that he used them to escape feeling inadequate and lonely, but he did not really need them because he could accomplish this by turning off the lights in his room while listening to music. His biggest problem was getting along with others; campus and social groups frightened him.

Jason was a borderline youngster—much like a 2-year-old, he was not yet ready to attend nursery school by himself. When the therapist suggested that he join an adult group she led, he agreed, saying he would probably feel safe in such a group. The therapist then told him that the group members would have to approve before he could join, that they would want to know his sex, age, and reasons for wanting to join. Jason said he needed to learn how to get along with others. He was intrigued by the idea that because he would be responsible for the fee, group therapy would be independent of his parents.

The Group

The open-ended group had been in existence for about two years and its seven members ranged in age from 24 to the early '30s. Some were married, and one had a child. It had a stable membership, a few changes occurring when members left, either because of resistance or because it was planned and accepted as therapeutically appropriate. The therapist discussed Jason's age carefully with the group members, who understood that many of their problems would seem strange to an 18-year-old. On the other hand, they noted that they were all struggling with feelings and events characteristic of a much younger age and wistfully wished they had received help earlier.

Jason dressed up for his first meeting. He talked incessantly, joked and made sarcastic comments. When asked what the group could do for him, he said that joining was the therapist's idea and he needed help in handling her. The other members quickly pointed out that his sarcasm was a two-edged sword: it hurt others and alienated him from people. It would be better if he listened more and joked less because they didn't want a clown in the group, which was hard-working. Slowly, as Jason listened to others speak, he began to discuss drugs, his new girlfriend, school, and work. When the men talked about problems with their wives, Jason said he wasn't there yet. When he talked about his experiences, the other members recalled their own adolescence, clarifying for him the difference that age makes, and explaining that people his age were expected to deal differently with sexual and social problems. But they also understood his use of drugs and his interest in music, and in some cases shared these experiences.

As Jason felt permission for his sexual interests, he began to dress like an adolescent, displaying pride in his body, wearing his shirt open to his navel, and exhibiting his hairy chest and silver necklace. He discussed his sexual problems, worrying because although he had erections, at times he could not ejaculate. This helped the older men to talk about their problems with premature ejaculation and about their wives' complaints. The group struggled with Jason during his first heterosexual relationship, pointing out his selfishness, then worrying because the girl did not care enough about him. When his girlfriend thought she was pregnant, they helped him plan to go with her to a physician. (She was not pregnant.)

Jason tended to be most critical of the youngest woman in the group. He accused her of being snobbish and flaunting her achievements, and the group encouraged him to examine his feelings about his sister. Jason was most impressed by a young married man who was not afraid to cry or show loving feelings and he listened intently when the man talked about his infant son. Jason then said he wanted more caring from his father. Later, he said he felt that maybe his father cared for him but did not know how to express such feelings to anyone.

There was always tension when a new member joined the group. At these times Jason regressed, going back to banter and superficial humor. When confronted with his behavior, he became quiet. On one occasion, however, he burst forth with devastating anger at himself because of his stupid behavior and was overwhelmed and depressed by his failure. When the therapist wondered aloud why he was angry only at himself, although the others had criticized him severely, Jason stormed out slamming doors. During the next meeting, he reported a big discovery. After the previous session, he said he had felt that maybe he was not so bad: "In fact, I'm a pretty good fellow." He had also discovered that if he smiled at people in the street, they smiled back at him. Having experienced and verbalized his rage and discovered that no one was hurt, he no longer had to defend himself by projecting his rage onto others.

Jason's passivity was related to his fear of aggression, primarily his own. One day, when the group questioned his lack of purpose and ideals, Jason said, "Why should I change? I have it easy; I'm where others want to be. My parents just live to retire and to do what I do. I like being cared for."

But Jason complained about the therapist's passivity. In individual sessions he asked her why she had not tried to prevent a member from leaving or to make everything better. The therapist in turn placed part of the responsibility on him. He talked of the group as being like a family; he cared for members and expressed his caring. He was particularly interested in the male members, whom he regarded as models.

As Jason grew older, he began to feel less afraid of activity and to remind the therapist that he was in charge of his therapy. His group fees had been increased from time to time and he eventually had accepted responsibility for paying for his individual sessions, which were also prorated until he reached age 21. At that point, he was able to pay for his own clothing and expenses as well as his therapy, but he still lived at home.

Jason experimented with leaving therapy, both group and individual, because he had friends and a steady relationship with a young woman. But he returned after a few months, saying he still had work to do.

The Older Member

After experimenting successfully with an adolescent who was now 20, the group decided to accept a 50-year-old man named Jim into the group. Although the members understood that Jim's age would make a difference, they were interested in the contributions an older man might make. The three women dressed up for this new and special man. Jim soon announced jauntily that he grew the largest marijuana plants in the country. He planted his crop in an empty lot and, at night, dressed in black, went out to tend to it. The group's rage and disappointment were clear; they called him a delinquent adolescent and told him to grow up. Jim was crestfallen, explaining that he always tried to be Jimmy the good guy, making jokes and wanting to be liked by everyone. He called this his Peter Pan act. The group helped him consider how and why this had come to be.

Jim was a successful businessman, but he felt like a failure. His business was never big enough. He was also too good to everybody, always behaving like Big Daddy. The eldest child in a large family and his mother's darling, he wanted to be more independent, able to think of his own interest. It was not until much later that he told the group he was an alcoholic.

Despite disparate ages, there were many similarities between Jim and Jason. Both were hungry for a father's attention; both felt smothered by and angry at women. In addition, Jason and Jim were creative, artistic, and unusually intelligent.

Jim had been born while his father was away in military service. Because of this, his mother had centered all of her attention on him. When her husband returned he was preoccupied with work and alcohol and there were financial struggles. Jim duplicated much of his father's history. He entered his father's business when he returned from service and married at a young age. But he was not able to have children, which he translated into feeling he had a small "business." He chose alcohol consumption as an escape from depression and feelings of inadequacy.

The group profited from Jim's repetition of his usual Big Daddy behavior; he worried about all of them. Thus they had a sense of being cared for, to which each reacted in an individually characteristic way. For example, one member's father had died when the son was 16; others, such as Jason, had fathers almost the same age as Jim. Yet Jim's struggle with his own problems, at times his insensitivity to his feelings and those of others, provided an opportunity for discussion of and anger at fathers' weaknesses. Jim joined in this ventilation.

The role of mothers and relationships between men and women easily flowed from concern with fathers, additionally stimulated by the woman leader and the group's mixed-sex composition. For Jim and others, relation to parents, gender role expectations, and performance began to be viewed from a multidimensional perspective. The group duplicated a family for all; for Jim it was particularly important that it was a family that considered his needs. Thus, when he acted against his own interests in the group or outside of it, he was helped to consider his actions from the double perspective of his own needs as well as others'. Jim's business became bigger; more important, he was able to make more money, feel more satisfied, and yet expend less effort so that he had more energy for his personal, family life.

It was customary for the group to review its collective and each individual's progress. After Jim had attended for a year, Jason remarked that the group that had helped him to be younger had helped Jim to become older and more mature.

In the history of this group, age was less significant than problems and the wish to be helped and to help. Later, when an older woman joined the group, Jason listened to her complaints and worries about her 20-year-old daughter and began to appreciate his parents' perspective. At the same time, the woman began to understand her daughter better as she listened to Jason. Differences of sex, problems, age, and even cultural and ethnic background enhanced the members' understanding and assisted their development.

CONCLUSION

Small groups tend to be replicas of the family, stimulating members to reenact family attitudes and behaviors. Although multiplicity, variability, and fragmentation of transferences are characteristic of any therapy group, one that contains members of widely different ages can be especially useful for older adolescents who have problems of separation from a pathological family and cannot use a peer group as a link to independence. This type of group can act as a transitional family, provide new identification, teach socialization, support entrance into adult roles, and enable the possibility of leaving the group when more age-appropriate and natural groups become of interest. The enabling of feeling and understanding helps the disturbed adolescent to engage in appropriate developmental tasks and personality growth, which then supports constructive separation from the primary family.

In turn, the adolescent can help older members recall the experiences and feelings of their younger days or feelings toward younger siblings. This enables growth as well as differentiation between the present and the past through retelling, rethinking, and refeeling. A heterogeneous group is most useful when it is combined with individual treatment because it permits varied reactions to the therapist both individually and in the group.

REFERENCES

Berkovitz, I. H., and Sugar, M. Indications and Contraindications for Adolescent Group Psychotherapy in M. Sugar (Ed.) *The Adolescent In Group and Family Therapy.* New York: Brunner/Mazel 1975.

Blos, P. The Second Individuation Process of Adolescence. *Psychoanalytic Study of the Child,* 1967, 22, 162–186.

Blos, P. The Split Parental Image in Adolescent Social Relations: An Inquiry Into Group Psychology. *Psychoanalytic Study of the Child,* 1976, 31, 7–34.

Buxbaum, E. *Troubled Children in a Troubled World.* New York: International Universities Press, 1970.

Davidson, H. The Role of Identification in the Analysis of Late Adolescents. In S. C. Feinstein and P. Giovacchini (Eds.) *Adolescent Psychiatry,* Vol. 3. New York: Basic Books, 1974.

Erikson, E. The Problem of Ego Identity. *Journal of the American Psychoanalytic Association,* 1956, 4, 56–121.

Erikson, E. *Childhood and Society.* New York: W. W. Norton and Co., 1963.

Freud, S. *Three Essays on the Theory of Sexuality.* Standard Edition 7:125, 1905.

Glatzer, H.T. The Working Alliance in Analytic Group Psychotherapy. *International Journal of Group Psychotherapy,* 1978, 28(2), 148, 161.

Laufer, M. A View of Adolescent Pathology. In S. C. Feinstein and P. Giovacchini (Eds.) *Adolescent Psychiatry,* Vol. 5. New York: Jason Aronson, 1977.

Lieberman, F., Caroff. P., and Gottesfeld, M. *Before Addiction.* New York: Behavioral Publications, 1973.

Meeks, J. E. Adolescent Development and Group Cohesion. In S. C. Feinstein and P. Giovaccchini (Eds.) *Adolescent Psychiatry,* Vol. 8. New York: Basic Books, 1974.

Slavson, S. *A Textbook in Analytic Group Psychotherapy.* New York: International Universities Press, 1964.

Spotnitz, H. A Comparison of Different Types of Group Psycchotherapy. In H. I. Kaplan and B. J. Saddock (Eds.) *Comprehensive Group Psychotherapy.* Baltimore: Williams and Wilkins Co., 1971.

HARRIET MAUER

10

Treatment of an Adolescent from a Multiproblem Family

MANY CLIENTS known to social work agencies suffer from chronic psychosocial dysfunction that oftens spans several generations. Because they do not readily seek out or accept help, these clients are typically labeled "hard to reach," or "unmotivated for treatment"— too often because the clinician's conception of treatment is limited.

The basic premise of this chapter is that so-called resistant adolescents and their families can respond to intervention if provided with services that are appropriate to their needs, stage of personality development, and life circumstances. Many clients with psychosocial impairment function at a primitive, preverbal level where they relate to themselves and the world through action, impulse discharge, and primary need gratification. Reflection, insight, and verbal communication are alien to them, and they are unable to trust in the most fundamental ways. Thus the therapist who invites or expects them to conceptualize or verbalize their thoughts and feelings may generate much anxiety, frustration, and feelings of inadequacy and humiliation, fostering a self-defeating process.

Adolescents who are in placement because of their own problems or those of their families present therapeutic difficulties. In addition to the usual problem of engaging and involving any adolescent in therapeutic work, these youngsters' complicated living situations in which they must relate to their natural families and their new environment compound the therapeutic task.

SPECIAL TASKS WITH ADOLESCENTS IN PLACEMENT

Attention to the environment of the client is an essential aspect of therapy. It is particularly important in work with children and adolescents, especially those who are in placement. Then the placement agency becomes part of their environment and, of necessity, must monitor all aspects of their lives. This includes natural families, education, health, and opportunities for socialization, and is consistent with the social work orientation and compatible with a major principle of ego psychology. When Heinz Hartmann (1958) introduced the concept of "an average expectable environment" as essential to growth, he noted that diagnostic assessment of a client's adaptiveness can be determined only in relation to his or her environment. Of necessity, this must affect the nature of the treatment plan.

Perlman (1972) noted that children in placement are "children in exile...(They) carry their absent parents alive within them and they fiercely fight and stonily resist being loved too much, too soon by strangers" (p. 137). The initial assessment that the family is not adequate for the adolescent, whatever the reason for this, immediately suggests a criticism and devaluation of the adolescent. By implication this is a denigration of part of the adolescent's self-image, of the internalized identifications, the roots, the essential components of identity and self. Such a reaction will occur even when the adolescent wishes to leave home. Thus a first task for children in placement will involve continued attention to the family. This means awareness of past and current interactions, psychological ties and conflicts relating to the family, and focused therapeutic work with the family. In the long run the family is the potential source of supportive networks and social relations throughout life. In this sense the family is more than the collected entity, more than the family system; it includes the individuals, the parents, and more important, siblings who should be assisted, wherever possible, to remain or to become continued sources of relatedness.

Beginning work with these families who may be very resistant to intervention, particularly if placement of a child is involved, is to provide emotional support and needed concrete services to counter early deficiencies and to foster trust and engagement. Only when they have learned to trust is it possible to attempt more sophisticated forms of treatment. As Lieberman (1979, p. 256) points out, concrete services are "too often the stepchild of clinical services." Yet communicating through the language of action—"doing things with people and sometimes even for them"—requires great skill and can foster trust and enable treatment. In addition, the act of providing concrete assistance to those who are overwhelmed and immobilized by chaos and crisis can serve as a model for more effective ways of coping and functioning.

A second task relates to education and academic achievement. These are crucial variables in the assessment and treatment in work with adolescents. Activities in school, more often than not, will reflect internal conflicts, symbolically linked to the family, identity, past experiences, and expectations for the self. For some there will be an investment in failure in an attempt to continue an identification with and loyalty to a family that often has consistently failed both itself and the child. Additionally, resistance to mastery may be connected to resistance to growing up because maturity may represent a burden and further unmanageable responsibilities.

For some adolescents, school represents a long-standing failure. This may be related to intellectual deficits, perceptual or neurological difficulties, deficient educational opportunities, etc. There are a variety of influences that impinge upon academic progress. Failure in this area leads to low self-esteem and tends to foster acting out instead of thinking out, because this latter ability has not been developed or encouraged. An important task of adolescence is the development of higher level thinking to further reflection instead of action, and future orientation as a replacement for the immediacy of action. It is in adolescence that the foundation for future work, opportunity, and often the very course of adult life is formulated. It is therefore essential that the educational progress of children in placement be carefully diagnosed, understood, and treated in a very *individualized* way.

A third task relates to therapeutic work with children in placement. Therapeutic intervention, or psychotherapy, is mandated by the circumstances that led to the present *abnormal* living, the abandonment inherent in being a "placed" child. The normative malleability of adolescence will shape much of the therapeutic thrust with these youngsters, modified by their circumstances and their idiosyncratic personalities and needs.

Adolescence is a period marked by both enormous receptivity and resistance to intervention and modification. According to Blos (1970), successful treatment of an adolescent client requires, first, an understanding of the developmental stage and, second, goals that are consonant with the client's individual situation and capacities. Although treatment is, of necessity, often fragmented and incomplete, it can provide a firm foundation for more intensive treatment at a later date, when the personality is better consolidated. Blos predicated this view on the fact that in adolescence certain defenses are necessary, appropriate, and adaptive, given the tenuous state of the ego; these defenses often serve as a preparation for and precondition of therapeutic work. He also noted that, although defended in some areas, the ego progresses in others. In the progressive stages of development each partial resolution results in developmental advances that in turn render the individual accessible to more profound interventions and deeper resolutions.

Given the diverse and divergent forces of adolescence, which on the one hand portend well for corrective intervention but on the other represent a major source of resistance, Steele (1957) suggests:

Most disturbed adolescents are eager for help and are very ready to use it when it is geared to what they need and not geared to what the adult feels the adolescent "should want" or "should have" at this time. This reiterates again that the therapist must be singularly free of emancipation problems of his own, and quite willing to go along with what seems to him, from a reality or long-term point of view, an irrelevant need at the time of therapy. The willingness of the therapist to lend himself to the adolescent along the adolescent's line of direction offers a basic, trusting confidence from an adult to a young person which has value far beyond the content of the interest itself. For instance, the adolescent's need to feel that his own interests and ideas, concerns and thoughts are of some basic worth and importance is translated by him into the basic feeling: "I am of worth and importance." This need is easily supported by the sympathetic therapist who is less concerned with the content of the interest per se than with the adolescent's right to have his own interests and to develop them along the lines that he sees fit...However, it goes without saying that such a vote of confidence must be governed by common sense, constructive boundaries which offset destructive and masochistic impulses in the adolescent (p. 155–156).

This statement touches on a major issue in work with adolescent clients. Their characteristic denial of dependency needs and vulnerability to regression are often the basis of their resistance to engagement. Additionally, resistance is in part an adaptive distancing device in the service of separation and dilution of the intensity of primary object ties. As a result, adolescents often view collaboration with an adult as helpless submission to authority or as loss of control. If their need to resist and protest is respected, they may be able to become involved in treatment without suffering a serious loss of self-esteem. Furthermore, exerting healthy resistance can strengthen the ego.

Related to these sources of resistance is the adolescent's disengagement or decathexis of libido from primary objects together with an increasing self-preoccupation and narcissism. The changing libido distribution is such that temporarily little may be available for reinvestment in outside objects. However, Anna Freud (1958) pointed out another important issue frequently encountered by therapists. Because of the urgency of their needs, limited tolerance for frustration, and their tendency to regard relationships as vehicles for wish fulfillment, adolescents may embrace treatment for emotional comfort rather than for insight or enlightenment. Nevertheless, this resistance to insight does not preclude therapeutic gains.

Recognizing the prevalent need among some clinicians to produce results, often for narcissistic reasons, Anthony (1974) proposed that "therapeutic activity" should be temporarily suspended in favor of "negative capability," which he defined as the capacity to endure ambiguity, doubt, and mystery without reaching for fact and reason. As a prerequisite for this capacity he suggested that therapists relinquish the grandiose idea that nothing will happen unless they make it happen. In this context,

Treatment becomes a place of postponement but not procrastination; of low pressure but not laissez-faire; of images, sensations, feeling, not action; a place for listening, observing, talking and experiencing, not deciding...(p. 30).

[The goal is] gradual closure of the therapeutically induced gap between "yes" and "no" to the point where "yes" becomes a positive affirmation and not an abject surrender and "no" become a positive negation and not an automatic rebelliousness....(p. 45).

Concerning the therapeutic techniques that are useful with adolescent clients, the general consensus is that flexibility and versatility are imperative. For example, Josselyn (1957) suggests that the choice of intervention should depend on the therapeutic tool that will strengthen the youngster's ego sufficiently to enable more effective dealing with internal and external strains and pressures and "what insight or experience will facilitate the healthy integration of the multiple drives and pressures to which the individual is exposed" (p. 38).

An important component of treatment with the adolescent is the therapist's role in establishing limits and controls. Given their healthy need to rebel and experiment in the face of impulsivity and limited abilities, adolescent clients need space, freedom, and tolerance combined with consistency, firmness, and control.

Case Example

In this case the primary client was an adolescent girl from a typical multiproblem family with multigenerational role-reversal patterns. Her treatment, which spanned four years, was guided by developmental and personality theory, involved her entire family, and included services ranging from concrete aid, environmental manipulations and interventions to traditional psychotherapeutic techniques. Principles of family therapy were also employed in this case.

Louise, a petite, attractive, well-groomed black youngster of high-average intelligence, was placed in a residence for adolescent girls at age 14 because her mother was unable to provide adequately for her developmental needs.

As a child, Louise's mother had lived on a farm in extreme poverty. Her own mother had died when Mrs. B. was 4, and until she could care for herself, she was passed from neighbor to neighbor. By the age of 8, she was given responsibility for the care of her three younger siblings. She experienced no consistent mothering herself and had little opportunity as a child to be dependent. At age 15 she gave birth to Louise, and at 16 married the child's father in the hope of escaping her oppressive home environment. She was ill-prepared for motherhood, but had four more children by the age of 22.

Although the marriage was marked by Mr. B.'s infidelities and periodic separations, he apparently cared about his family and was a stabilizing influence on his wife and children. When Louise was 7 and the youngest child had been born, Mr. B. left the family permanently, moving south with a woman friend. Although his subsequent contacts with the family were sporadic, he contributed to their support and served as a stabilizing element in Mrs. B.'s life. A year after leaving home, he died suddenly—an event that was a major turning point for her. Before his death she had maintained a positive job record, had provided the basic necessities for her children, and had given them a substantial amount of mothering. After he died she began to drink heavily, was promiscuous, and exhibited erratic, volatile, and unstable behavior countered by periods of devotion to her children.

When Louise was 11 (the age at which she began to menstruate), she saw her mother stab and kill her lover, who had also been a benign paternal figure to the children. Mrs. B. was convicted of manslaughter and was sentenced to five years' probation. She subsequently lost her job and began receiving public assistance. Shortly thereafter the family's apartment was destroyed by fire, and she and the children moved into a grossly inadequate apartment.

Although treatment was a condition of her probation, this had not been enforced. She continued to drink heavily and became even more erratic and unstable. As a result Louise had to assume the role of mother, not only to her siblings, but to her mother as well.

One evening Mrs. B. beat Louise and locked her out of the house. The child sought help from the police and was eventually placed in long-term care. After the mother signed the commitment papers, she went into seclusion and would not respond to agency outreach efforts.

Placement Initially, Louise seemed an enigma. She was vague and evasive about the reasons for her request for placement. She was restless, agitated, and in constant motion. Her thinking was hysterical, dissociative, diffuse, and unfocused. She vacillated between verbal overproduction and mute withdrawal. Her ability to test reality was often tenuous; she exhibited bizarre behavior and fantasied excessively. The fantasies were grotesque and violent in nature. Her moods vacillated between brittle withdrawal and explosive anger or manic expansiveness. She was somewhat phobic, particularly about violence, attack, or intrusion; tended to somatize; and suffered from nightmares and other sleep disturbances. Her interpersonal relationships were guarded and tentative and had a schizoid quality. She appeared to be a loner and was perceived by others as strange.

During relatively calm periods she was superficially outgoing, self-dramatizing, and vivacious and played the role of comic entertainer. As a result of her alert mind, wit, and facility with words, she could elicit positive but wary regard from peers and adults. She also achieved many secondary gains by assuming the roles of victim, martyr, and scapegoat.

Initially, though Louise refused to attend regularly scheduled therapy sessions, she would drop into the office after school on the pretext of asking for candy. Then Louise began to use these impromptu sessions to chat and ventilate, but she avoided intimate or emotionally charged material. Frequently, she embarked on what seemed to be agitated flights into fantasy. Recognizing the child's ambivalence, the worker avoided probing and merely demonstrated her availability. Louise became calmer and her primary process productions decreased; she could discuss neutral issues coherently and with appropriate affect.

Louise began to make oblique references to her concern about her family. She admitted she visited her family, but said that her mother had bound her to secrecy. She admitted to stealing food from the residence for them and that she was unable to ignore her mother's pleas for money. Mrs. B. was still drinking heavily, and Louise felt responsible, saying: "I'm the only one that can make her stop. She listens to me. She needs me home."

Louise strenuously resisted attachments and made tentative requests to return home. She seemed trapped in a situation of profound role reversal reminiscent of her mother's childhood. She was experiencing much turmoil, feeling she had abandoned her family. In fact, major themes that emerged were her inordinate guilt, sense of responsibility, resentment, and rage at her burden, and were expressed through depression, regression, self-punishment, and tentative efforts at sabotaging placement.

Family It was evident that Louise's functioning was integrally linked with her family and that disproportionate amounts of energy were consumed by conflicts in this sphere. Neither her functioning nor her treatment could be separated from that of her family. This was a family characterized by fluid roles and boundaries and pathological overinvolvement. It was isolated and insulated, with no community or familial supports. But there were also positive, benign ties that needed safeguarding. Additionally, four younger children remained at home and at risk.

Mrs. B. thwarted all attempts to reach the family. However, one evening the mother called, insisting that Louise must come home because of an emergency; Mrs. B. was drunk, and had locked herself out of her apartment. The worker, Louise, and a locksmith came to assist the mother who seemed stunned by the worker's availability and attention. She apologized for her former lack of cooperation and agreed to visit the agency the next day. Regular visits to the home ensued.

This encounter, which took place in the child's presence, was critical. The experience of seeing two individuals, whom she perceived as vying for her loyalty, acting in apparent harmony seemed to stimulate integration, demonstrated by a slowly decreasing tendency to split, fragment, and compartmentalize.

Mrs. B. seemed extremely immature, dependent, profoundly depressed, and capable of volatile paranoid behavior, especially when drinking. When intoxicated, she hallucinated, but her decompensation seemed related to alcohol rather than to an underlying psychosis. She was caring, warm, likeable, and intelligent. The children, although extremely guarded and cautious, were warm and demonstrated the capacity to give to one another. They had adequate social values, and seemed bright and oriented to education.

The mother was overwhelmed by practical matters such as housing and finances. She was helped to move into a more adequate apartment and to work out problems involving welfare, Medicaid, and budgeting. Gradually Mrs. B. was able to talk openly about emotional problems. She was extremely upset about her daughter's placement; she was concerned about her own drinking problem and her inability to meet her children's needs or control the four younger ones, who were beginning to misbehave. Her overriding concern, however, was whether the worker would use this information against her to remove her children. She also suffered from overwhelming guilt about having committed murder.

There was no miraculous recovery. Mrs. B. made some gains, but her needs were enormous. Often the worker would find her drunk and paranoid. Then Mrs. B. would regard the worker as the enemy who was depriving her of her daughter. There would be fits of explosive verbal abuse, then apologies and expressions of gratitude. But the family situation remained precarious; the four children were still at risk and Louise's behavior began to deteriorate.

Temporary placement was introduced to the mother as a needed reality but also as an opportunity for the mother to have time to concentrate on her own needs. The initial reaction was one of anger, and feelings of being betrayed. However, she became receptive to a plan for the children to enter a small group home that was near the mother's home. Family sessions prepared the way for this placement. The mother committed herself to an inpatient alcoholism program and followed through, becoming actively involved, after her discharge, with the social worker at the group home. As she explored her own feelings and experimented with new ways of coping, she learned to be a more effective parent as well as a more self-reliant adult. She became active in parents' groups, began earning her high-school equivalency diploma, and planned to enroll in a vocational training program.

There was close collaboration among all therapists, with participation in joint and family sessions. Eventually discharge plans were initiated for the younger children.

Treatment of the adolescent Louise presented as a youngster with adolescent strengths and impulses but with serious developmental arrest. The immediate and ongoing task was to provide an "average expectable environment" to meet defective and normal developmental needs. Placement combined with intervention in all areas of her life was focused toward building and reinforcing ego-adaptive capacities while reducing external sources of stress.

Once in a protected setting, engagement of the adolescent had to be achieved. Louise was highly anxious, ambivalent, and resistant. In the service of engagement, the worker made herself available while providing space, respecting the child's defenses, and allowing her the opportunity to resist, protest, deny, ventilate without prematurely imposing a treatment agenda. Emphasis was to foster a nonintrusive, nonthreatening alliance. The effort to engage the family was not only to provide for the needs of the others, but also a mechanism for reducing Louise's stress and freeing her to utilize placement. While Louise herself employed mechanisms of distancing from her family, avoiding some demands through retreat to illness and acting out, the social worker and child-care staff assumed the role of temporary buffer. As Louise became reassured in her trust that the agency would support her family, and as the family decreased its demands on her, she was gradually able to relax her defenses, attach herself to others, and accept emotional supplies. Eventually the family and Louise were better able to establish their own limits and achieve more effective boundaries.

Intellectually, Louise tested within the high-average range, clearly an asset and ally in the therapeutic endeavor. Her elementary school record was average, but she had a significant, albeit conflicted, investment in education and mastery in this sphere. However, upon entering junior high school, which coincided with placement, she experienced problems in school. She truanted, was defiant with teachers, was isolated from peers, failed to complete school assignments, and was distractable and apathetic. Eventually it was discovered that when truant she was visiting home.

Louise was quickly enrolled in a mini school in an effort to reduce stress and to provide a more protective, supportive school environment. This individualized school approach, collaboratively coordinated with treatment, enabled the child slowly to experience a sense of achievement, mastery, and heightened self-esteem.

Initially Louise was minimally capable of reflection or introspection and was not invested in formal treatment. Despite recurrent resistance, Louise was eventually able not only to tolerate more contact with the worker, but to initiate contact. She became more open, direct, related, and capable of discussing painful emotional issues.

As is typical in adolescence, Louise struggled with issues of dependency–independency. She often assumed a pseudo-mature, pseudo-independent stance, denying her own dependency, as if fearful of regression to a state of infantile fusion and helplessness. When her family became more stablized and represented less of a real external threat, it became apparent that Louise had a significant investment in family crisis; it made her feel needed and loved, and also served as a defense against looking at her needs independent of the family. She was helped to face this changed external reality and encouraged to look within and eventually to feel her sense of loss, sadness, ambivalence, and anger concerning her family's improved situation. "They don't care about me. They only wanted me around when they needed something." In time she relinquished her rigid defensive posture and permitted herself some appropriate regression in the service of growth.

Coinciding with her insight into the secondary gains provided by the familial crisis and neediness, she was further encouraged to develop new means of coping, new tools to mastery and achievement. With increasing delight and gratification in age-appropriate tasks such as school, peers, and a part-time job, Louise's investments and energies began to shift. She was becoming more comfortable with calm and stability, enjoying the newly found satisfaction of expending energy on her own needs and independent interests and accomplishments.

Louise's heightened sense of mastery served to modify her perception of herself and society. Initially she viewed herself as a passive victim in a malevolent world. Eventually she began to see herself as a worthwhile, resourceful, capable person who could have an impact on the environment.

With Louise's progress, her denial, retreat from reality, and tendency to withdraw into fantasy lessened. Hartmann (1958) viewed fantasy as a form of regression in the service of ego. While initially the degree of fantasy production was alarming, in retrospect it seems to have served an adaptive function, providing temporary retreat from an intolerable reality in order better to prepare for the eventual mastery of reality.

One of the tasks of placement had been to help Louise master the skills required for independent living. By her junior year of high school, she began to plan actively for her future. Following a long, painful struggle, she decided to attend college in upstate New York, which she was able to do successfully. But going to college represented white, middle-class values and standards that both appealed to her and worried her.

Placement had provided an abrupt and dramatic exposure to new and alien realities and possibilities. Throughout the placement period, the period of her adolescence, Louise was engaged in an active struggle to define who she was. She expressed a painful and ambivalent wish to counter her identification with poverty, violence, the ghetto, her alcoholic mother, her mother the murderer, all sources of shame. Yet these were her roots and a part of her that she could not betray. While recognizing Louise's need for new objects of identification and counteridentification, the agency was equally bound to safeguard her roots, her familial, cultural, and racial identifications and affiliations. Ultimately the agency's involvement with the entire family provided Louise with an opportunity to be proud of her mother.

Shortly before Louise left for college, Louise and her mother discussed their vocational choices, each representing for the other a model of autonomy and self-reliance as well as a source of support and inspiration. Later, Louise commented to the worker:

Isn't it strange? We used to talk about Mom's being too dependent on me, about me acting like her mother and her being the child. It's good now coming to her for advice about my future. Yet she still needs me, but it's not like before. We're alike in many ways now. She wants my opinion. She seems frightened and a little lost, but it's good to help her this way. She's going to make it. I think I will too.

Mrs. B., in turn, expressed her pride in Louise:

I never had a mother who taught me. I don't need a mother now, but I'm learning a lot from Louise. I've learned a lot from you and the other social workers who've helped me and the children. I'm catching up. I want Louise and the children to be proud of me. I feel I'm somebody now—not just a drunk and an ex-con.

CONCLUSIONS

Psychotherapy is essential for adolescents who are in placement. The reality of removal from home is usually preceded by unsettling and often pathological experiences that make placement necessary. This threatens the continuity and security essential for the enabling of adolescent tasks related to ego growth and mastery, completion of internal work relating to identity and identifications, issues of dependence–independence, and preparation for the future. However, psychotherapy will not be accepted by these youngsters if it occurs independent of their day-to-day struggles. They are not motivated to visit a psychotherapist.

The therapeutic work must be an integral part of their placement experience, formally structured into the new living experience. It needs also to be accompanied by intensive involvement with their families and the use of a variety of appropriate, well-timed concrete services and environmental manipulations. Above all, there must be flexibility, versatility, and patience on the part of the therapeutic agents.

REFERENCES

Anthony, E. J. Between Yes and No: The Potentially Neutral Area Where the Adolescent and His Therapist Can Meet. *Psychosocial Process*, Fall 1974.

Blos, P. *The Young Adolescent: Clinical Studies*. New York: Free Press, 1970.

Freud, A. Adolescence. *The Psychoanalytic Study of the Child*, 1958, 13.

Hartmann, H. *Ego Psychology and the Problem of Adaptation*. New York: International Universities Press, 1958.

Josselyn, I. Psychotherapy of Adolescents at the Level of Private Practice. In B. Balser (Ed.) *Psychotherapy of the Adolescent*. New York: International Universities Press, 1957.

Lieberman, F. *Social Work with Children*. New York: Human Sciences Press, 1979.

Perlman, H. H. Children in Exile. *Social Work*, 1972, 22, 137–139.

Steele, E. Discussion of Chapters IV, V, VI. In B. Balser (Ed.) *Psychotherapy of the Adolescent*. New York: International Universities Press, 1957.

CRAYTON E. ROWE, JR.

Narcissism and Hyperaggressiveness: A Study of Hyperaggressive Borderline Children

CHILDREN WHO ARE SUBJECTED to multiple deprivations as the result of disorganizing ghetto conditions, extreme poverty, violence, and inconstancy frequently suffer developmental deficits that may be expressed behaviorally through hyperaggressiveness. Such behavior, although reflective of internal disability, may often be in response to external disorganization (Pine, 1974). The hyperaggressive behavior appears and is experienced by others as uncontrolled aggressive behavior.

This chapter presents the findings of a staff study group at the University Settlement Consultation Center, a psychiatric clinic serving a predominantly Hispanic and black population on the Lower East Side of New York. The treatment of 23 hyperaggressive borderline children was followed from the time of referral to the time of termination. The findings suggest that instead of uncontrolled behavior, these children show a high degree of control, but reflect ideation of a defensive, grandiose, and omnipotent image. Such an image serves as a stabilizing identity for children living in extremely threatening environments. This milieu encourages aggressive behavior because of a high tolerance for aggression and

Appreciation is expressed to Paul Mayglothling and Richard Holm for their clinical contributions to this chapter.

151

because it exposes the children to fixed expectations of continuously having to defend themselves from responses that tend to disorganize their personality systems.

Treatment that focuses on improving the child's behavior through establishing a conflict-solving, working alliance will be perceived as a threat to the child's identity, stability, and existing personality organization. Such an approach prematurely eliminates needed tension-producing conflicts and bypasses the preliminary work that must be accomplished with the narcissistically damaged child.

HYPERAGGRESSION

The term "hyperaggressiveness" is used in a descriptive sense and refers to hyperactive behavior that is predominantly influenced by instinctual discharges. While all hyperaggressive children can be considered hyperactive, the reverse is not necessarily true in that hyperactivity in children may be the result of a variety of factors. Ross and Ross (1976) define the hyperactive child as one "who consistently exhibits a high level of activity in situations in which it is clearly inappropriate, is unable to inhibit his activity on command, often appears capable of only one speed of response, and is often characterized by other physiological learning and behavioral symptoms and problems" (pp. 11–12).

The literature defines hyperaggressiveness in children as *uncontrolled* aggression occurring because of several factors. These include unusual drive endowment (Alberts, Neubauer, and Weil, 1956; De Hirsch, 1975; Fries and Woolf, 1953), defective body image (Blos, 1960), frustration of available avenues of discharge through motility (Bettelheim and Sylvester, 1949; Mittelmann, 1957; Pavenstedt, 1956), regression to motor level of development (Mittelmann, 1954), conflictual relationships resulting in immature ego development (Beres, 1952; Fries and Woolf, 1953; Geleerd, 1946; Holder, 1968; Rank and MacNaughton, 1950), and drive diffusion (Eissler, 1971).

In contrast, the behavior of the children under study revealed a high degree of control. For example, rarely did these children injure themselves, even though they explosively leaped and climbed to dangerous precipices and ran full speed through rooms full of furniture. The skillfull maneuvering, balancing, and destructively accurate throwing and hitting gave rise to the impression that the behavior was, instead, a manifestation of a highly primitive and aggressive form of identification.

One of Anna Freud's (1973) major contributions, "Identification with the Agressor," clarifies how aggressive forms of identifications can result from efforts by the child to turn passively experienced traumatic situations into active, pleasurable ones. She points out that the child may identify only with the perceived attributes of the aggressor (or with the aggression itself), and not necessarily with the person of the aggressor. The introjected characteristics of the anxiety object can assume archaic symbolic forms. This process helps the child to defend against narcissistic mortification.

Fixations in development can occcur on infantile levels of omnipotence, if the child becomes involved in fierce struggles for power. Fantasies of omnipotence (omnipotence of thought and magic of words) are retained to protect the child against feelings of helplessness (Pumpian-Mindlin, 1969). Kohut (1966, 1968, 1971, 1977) through his study of narcissistic pathology in adult patients, also postulates that fixations can occcur on primitive narcissistic levels of development as a result of traumatic experiences with adult figures. He suggests that fixations take place on what he describes as the grandiose self and an image of the idealized parent image.

The following vignettes highlight a treatment approach that is based on the supposition that the child's hyperaggressive behavior is a manifestation of a primitive form of identification.

The Case of Robbie

Robbie, 9 years old, was referred by his school (where he was in the third grade) because he was unmanageable. His aggressive outbursts and general agitation, apparent from first grade on, led to frequent class disruptions. Poor concentration and frustration tolerance severely interfered with his learning, and as a result he was below grade level in every area of his studies. At times, he would suddenly leave the classroom and wander around the school building.

Robbie was the youngest of five boys who were born approximately one year apart. He lived with his mother and brothers in a small, overcrowded two-bedroom apartment. His father had left the home when Robbie was 2, which made it necessary for his mother to obtain welfare assistance. The mother, who had borne her first child at 13, described her life as overwhelming from that time on. She could not tolerate the noise and overcrowded conditions with which she had to live. She felt "swamped" by her children with their constant questions, demands, etc. She frequently would punish them physically by hitting and/or leaving them unattended for several hours at a time. The mother was seen only once despite repeated efforts to involve her.

There had been frequent struggles with Robbie regarding toilet training. His independent, grandiose, and exhibitionistic behavior was met with punitive control. Inadequate living space, primal scene exposure, plus a series of separations from surrogate parental figures, were only some of the deprivations suffered by this child.

Robbie was seen in the office of the school guidance counselor. When he was introduced, he said nothing but began to run about in an intense and aggressive fashion. At the same time he would quickly pick up various games, puzzles, etc., and put them down with a sweeping motion of his arm, almost as if to indicate he had magically engaged in and completed these activities. The first treatment concern was to reflect the perceived emotional quality of the child's experience. The primary process quality of the following opening dialogue captured the archaic and diffuse quality of the child's grandiosity:

Therapist: (with a quick thrust of his arm): "Swissssh."
Robbie: "Zoom-zoom-zoom he zoom."

Following that exchange, Robbie looked at the therapist for the first time since he was introduced. In speaking, he referred to himself in the third person and continued his maneuvering throughout the room and magically gesturing. His movements seemed faster, and he covered a greater area as he circled the room. The therapist sensed he was not sufficiently empathic with the totality of Robbie's experience. His faster movements and his covering a larger area of the room had an additional omnipresent quality of being everywhere at once. With a sweeping motion of his arms, the therapist attempted to reflect this aspect of Robbie's grandiosity: "Zoom-zoom-zoom-zoom."

Robbie smiled and his speed decreased. He began to refer to the therapist as "he" and included him in his play, in much the same manner as he did the toys. He walked up to the therapist and ritualistically waved his arms as if he had completed some meaningful interaction. Occasionally he placed a toy in the therapist's hands and continued his magical gesturing. Then at one point he seemed to become calm. He turned away and quietly left the room, returning to class by himself.

As the therapist continued to reflect the quality of Robbie's grandiose self-experience, his hyperaggressive behavior became less continuous and pervasive and more related to specific situations where there was a break in the relationship. He would always become aggressive in his play at the end of the session or would run from the interviewing room back to class.

After a while, Robbie began to call the therapist by name and at times asked questions about his personal life. Now the therapist was becoming a separate individual outside the configuration of "he." With this, communication improved. The therapist was able to make rudimentary clarifications of the connection between the child's grandiose, aggressive behavior and the break in relationship at the end of sessions. For example, during one of these outbursts, the therapist said: "I think, Robbie, you are feeling big and strong at this very minute—just when I said we have to stop." Robbie ignored this, but at the following session when the same thing was said, Robbie replied, "Sure."

Eventually Robbie said he had "no good feelings" when he had to leave. These "no good feelings" were sensed as intense anxiety responses and were distinct from his powerful "he" experiences. Now Robbie's aggressive behavior was connected with his experiencing "no good feelings." "Robbie, when you have those 'no good feelings' you become zoom-zoom strong—and zoom away from those 'no good feelings'." Again Robbie seemed to ignore the clarification, but he did not become aggressive at the end of the session, nor did he run out of the room. At the beginning of the next session he reported that he had "no good feelings" today with his teacher and zoomed, zoomed with her. Though he was unable to speak of the specifics, his behavior in the classroom began to improve. He was able to concentrate and stay seated for longer periods. He was able to take directions and no longer left the classroom.

Gradually the archaic quality of Robbie's grandiose ideations gave way to more normal and less defensive configurations. The child imagined himself as a specific football hero, a quarterback, who was able to help his team to victory. He took delight in playing football games with the therapist and wanted to learn from him how to pass and catch. He no longer related to the therapist as "he" or played in a ritualistic and stereotypical way.

At one point Robbie suddenly regressed to his previous hyperaggressive behavior. He refused to take directions from the teacher and became generally disruptive. He could not concentrate on his studies and frequently was truant. In treatment Robbie once again played out the powerful "he" who could magically exert control. He introduced a theme of a "killer monster." Home visits revealed evidence that Robbie was repeatedly raped by an adult male. After interventions effectively reduced the threat of further violence, aggressive behavior began to diminish, and Robbie alternated between projections of "killer monster," "he," and expressions of affectionate feelings for the therapist, whom he once again began to call by name. For example, he left the following note at the end of one session: "Monster—you monster—eat you up—kill you. Love, Robbie."

Many things occurred simultaneously. There was better concentration in class and in sessions the "monster" and "he" ideations disappeared. Robbie began to play football and he threw winning passes to the therapist just in time before huge imaginary tacklers knocked him down. He began to be strongly competitive, engaging the therapist in a variety of sports and other games such as checkers and monopoly. Each time Robbie lost he would angrily challenge the therapist to play again. A greater capacity for object relatedness and an ability to express his anger directly toward a specific object marked another significant step in treatment. He arrived at a point where he could be helped to explore, in a limited way, the transference aspects of his responses to the therapist and those of the fantasies that emerged in his play.

But these developments also produced an awareness of the many massive and unresolvable conflicts in his home situation. He looked and acted depressed and began to stay away from treatment. He asked to discontinue. He said he no longer wished to speak about his problems at home, which he described as "making me too sad to sleep." He wanted the therapist to be his "best friend" and to take him on outings and play sports outside the office situation. Formal treatment was terminated and instead Robbie's request was honnored and the therapist and the child used the athletic facilities of the Settlement to play many sports. Robbie talked only limitedly of his conflicts, but was able to sustain his improved functioning and reach his grade level until the family moved away from the district.

The Case of Frankie

Frankie, 8 years of age, referred by his school guidance counselor, was described as a child in "perpetual motion". He disrupted his third-grade class by walking around and picking fights with his classmates. He had a history of hyperactivity and poor school work; he was approximately two grades below average in math and reading. Psychological testing indicated that he was of average intelligence but had severe disturbances in reality testing, impulse control, and concept formation. He was diagnosed as a borderline child with the possibility of an underlying schizophrenic process. His mother agreed to therapy for her son, but she was not interested in any ongoing discussions, either about herself or her family.

Frankie was the second oldest of six children who were approximately a year and a half apart in age. His older brother lived outside the country with the father, who had separated from the mother when Frankie was born. By the time Frankie was 2½ his mother, age 17, had given birth to two other children by different men, each of whom stayed only a short time and refused to support her. On welfare, and living in extreme poverty in a small three-and-a-half room railroad flat, the mother described her life as "unbearable." When she felt overwhelmed by the demands of the children, she would leave them unattended for several hours at a time. She described Frankie as having been a physically healthy child who became "stubborn like his father" when he began to walk; he would not obey her. She toilet trained him by the age of 1½ by spanking him and yelling when he soiled. She recalled she had no one to help her with her children and expected Frankie not to give her trouble. When he was 3, she became pregnant with her fifth child. Again she received no support and the man visited only sporadically. Then she physically began to punish Frankie more frequently because he "fought" with his younger brother, now 2 years of age. She became especially enraged when the boys would explore the apartment, open drawers, etc. She thought Frankie a bad influence and wished he could live with his father. When, after the birth of her fifth child, welfare provided larger living quarters, life became a little better. However, Frankie's independent behavior still met with strict control. Frankie was exposed to sexual scenes as well as experiencing sudden separations from parental figures.

When Frankie was introduced to the therapist he appeared dazed, as if in a trancelike state. Then he began to move quickly about the room in a zigzag fashion, but his eyes were glazed and did not focus on any objects. His speed increased as he maneuvered skillfully around chairs and other furniture, without touching or bumping into them. However, his body movements seemed robotlike. When the therapist attempted to talk to him, Frankie contin-

ued his zigzag movements, and intensified them when there were
continued efforts at talking. Only when the therapist, with a quick
zigzag motion of his hands, uttered a loud swishing sound, did
Frankie react; he looked quickly back over his shoulder and began
to smile and soon stopped his running. Springing forward, he circled a small chair, stopped, and looked at the worker. Now. attempt-
ing to capture the emotional quality and pattern of the child's
movements, the worker made a short straight motion with his arm
and a circular one, accompanied by the swishing sound. Frankie
smiled and went through a third maneuver, which was again captured in sound and movement.

Frankie now seemed calmer. He walked up to the therapist, and
stared at him as if he wanted to say something, but instead turned
toward the door and began to switch the light on and off. He
switched the light on, yelled "Flash," and disappeared to return to
class.

Treatment continued. Each time the therapist reflected Frankie's
magical grandiose actions, the child smiled, but said nothing.
Though few words were exchanged in therapy, in class Frankie
began to participate more in verbal discussions. As he was able to
stay in his seat for longer periods, his disruptive behavior diminished.

Treatment involved a series of maneuvers with light switches,
balls that were thrown to be caught but not returned, toys that were
piled on and in the therapist's space, jumping, etc. Eventually Frankie took a puzzle from the toys he had been piling together and
asked: "You help me put this puzzle together?" For approximately
20 minutes and until the end of the session, the child worked on the
puzzle, seeming to welcome the worker's participation. With this,
Frankie began viewing the therapist more as a separate individual
outside his grandiose world of maneuvers and he began communicating in words.

It was now possible to make rudimentary clarifications that
connected Frankie's aggressive behavior and his experiencing states
of helplessness. Eventually Frankie was able to describe in some
detail his feeling "funny" and "frozen" when the therapist ended the
sessions (Frankie reacted explosively to ending of sessions). With
this, hyperaggressive behavior in class diminished dramatically,
fighting decreased, and school work was completed and improved.
He, too, became interested in a variety of sports. He took special
delight in playing out complicated dramas where he was a famous
sword fighter who rescued helpless and hurt boys and girls from
drunken robbers.

Frankie was able to relate his play only limitedly to his life situation. He spoke in a general way of being hurt by his mother and by drunken men who hit his mother and him. With such awareness there would follow a regressive return to maneuvering behavior. He could identify feeling "frozen" when thinking of his home and made some connection between feeling "frozen" and feeling like "flash." As the child became increasingly aware of the unchanging nature of the home situation, he seemed depressed, and began to miss sessions. He wanted to restructure the formal treatment into a big brother relationship. Again the Settlement House was used, and in addition Frankie was helped to become involved in its after-school activities. He was able to achieve grade-level performance in school.

DISCUSSION

Robbie's "he" and Frankie's "flash" symbolize the destructive intrusions that pervaded the children's life situations. They were "aggressor" identifications with cumulative disorganizing experiences and the hyperaggressive behavior was an expression of these self-images. Initially there could be no investment in any activity that would disrupt these powerful experiences. As a consequence, the whole range of development of high-order ego and superego function was severely hampered; both children performed below level and evidenced no guilt or remorse about their destructive behavior.

The children experienced a constant threat of unchecked anxiety flooding as a result of defective development of tension and anxiety regulatory functions. The accruing of these functions is discussed by Tolpin (1971), who focuses on the separation–individuation phase as a critical time when traumatic narcissistic disappointments can lead to maintaining defective internalizations and structural defects. Her study supports Kohut's formulations and follows upon research by Mahler (1966, 1968), Spitz (1950), and Winnicott (1953).

The threat to Robbie of experiencing "no good feelings" and Frankie's feeling "frozen" acted as a continuous and indiscriminate signal, which resulted in the hypercathexis of the narcissistically stabilizing aggressor images. Retaliation and the enforcement of proscribed behavior by teachers and other adult figures only served further to threaten the children with the loss of the sustaining ideations and ensued in destructive power struggles.

In treatment it was necessary to capture and empathically reflect the primary process experience and its omnipresent quality. Only then could the therapist be included within the child's projected boundaries of his self-object world, and could he be related to as one of the child's many inanimate self-objects. The establishment of an empathic relationship provides these children with mirroring reponses that were previously unavailable or faulty. As a result they are then able to view their therapists as nonthreatening and include them within the boundaries of the primitive self-object world. Each termination of a session disrupted the narcissistically stabilizing self-experience; explosive outbursts were expressions of recovered grandiose ideations.

Treatment helped sustain these children through these necessary separations. In time they were able to verbalize their dreaded anxiety experiences and come to an awareness of simple cause-and-effect connections. As a result there was a bit-by-bit reduction in previous fixed expectations of continuously having to defend themselves from disorganizing responses. Reductions in these expectations were accompanied by a decreased need for defensive archaic ideations. This enabled seeing the therapist as a separate individual; primitive forms of identifications then gave way to more reality-oriented identifications with sports heroes. Concurrently, aggression abated and play became more of a recreation of specific object-related conflicts as in the usual sense of play therapy.

For the most part these children have made reasonable psychological adaptations within the context of a social and cultural environment that has been skewed and deformed by the complexities of mixed cultural influences and unchanging poverty conditions. It is, however, this same disorganizing environment, with its high tolerance for aggressive behavior, that has provided avenues of stablizing, defensive, grandiose expression. Also, evidence suggest that mothers show considerable affection for their children during the early stages of separation—individuation and before the children become more physically independent. It is perhaps these two factors that may well have prevented more serious disturbances.

It is important that treatment take into account the need for these children to maintain their grandiose ideations. If, however, the assumption is made that the hyperaggressive behavior evidenced by these children is a result of a breakthrough of drive forces, it is likely there would be a focus on diminishing or controlling the child's powerful behavior. Beginning discussions that focus on establishing a conflict-solving, working alliance and attempts to engage in secondary dialogue are experienced as threats to the sustaining ideations and exacerbate hyperaggressive behavior.

The child who has developed a more substantial ego organization experiences excessive tension and conflict as potentially destablizing. Therefore, in therapy these children will play out conflictual situations to reduce conflict. Therapy has as a goal the uncovering of the nature of pathological object relationships and the effects these relationships have on the child's psychosexual development. Analysis results in the widening of the child's ego capacities and the overall advancement of the child's development.

In contrast, the children studied had remained fixed on archaic forms of identifications that were defensive against basic defects in the formation of an individuated self. They utilized the play situation to maintain their stabilizing, tension-producing, narcissistic ideations. Therapy focused on helping these children become aware of the defensive relationship between experiencing primitive narcissistic states and experiencing states of helplessness. As a result, defensive fixations were loosened and the unfinished process of separation–individuation was set in motion within the context of an empathic relationship.

The accruing of new ego capacities and enhanced feelings of self-esteem increased the children's capacity for the exploration of previously repressed conflicts and confusions. Their play became more and more a recreation of specific object-related conflicts as in the usual sense of play therapy. Therefore, play materials, dolls, games, etc., were utilized more in the service of mastering specific anxiety-provoking situations and less in the service of maintaining powerful narcissistic ideations. The children showed an increased ability to verbalize the conflicts they experienced at home and in school. In general their behavior became more age appropriate and socially accepted.

It was at this point that formal treatment was broken off by the children after they accurately perceived the conflictual nature of their home situation and their inability to effect sufficient changes in it.

The hopelessness felt upon coming to that level in treatment where the child is able to view the punitive home situation objectively was vividly and pathetically expressed by one 9-year-old boy. This child, after two years of treatment, had reached a point where he began playing out fantasies of a well-know champion boxer who could dodge all the blows from an imaginary opponent. The therapist, in an attempt to relate his play to the child's life situation, wondered if the child sometimes felt someone might hit him. The boy began to cry and revealed how his father hit him that morning. He immediately ran from the room. Before he disappeared into the hallway, he turned and yelled that no one loved him. This child returned to sessions only after the therapist agreed not to speak about his family.

Needless to say, it would be better if parents became actively involved in correcting the many problems. While concentrated efforts are made to reach out to them, these efforts require considerable time—time these children don't have. Delay in treating the children as an effort to coordinate treatment with the family, etc., can only lead to worsening conditions.

As previously stated, the children studied wished to maintain the sustaining empathic relationship they had formed with the therapist, but as a friend or as a substitute parent. Some would ask the therapist to be a "second" father or mother and offered to buy candy or food for the therapist as an inducement. Other children established friendly relationships with group program leaders at the Settlement and/or with peers who could provide a similar empathic relationship. Frequently children became attached to older siblings. One child, after four years of treatment, became aware of the unchanging nature of his punitive situation at home, where he lived alone with his father. He made a request to his father to live with an older brother who resided outside the country. His father agreed to the arrangement and planned to see his son on a periodic basis. Follow-up showed that this child was able to maintain his improved functioning and to become involved in a number of interests previously unavailable to him.

As with the above child, follow-up with families and school shows that all children are able to maintain improved functioning. Follow-up occurs as an ongoing and natural process as children who terminate formal treatment usually keep some contact with the therapist and/or other personnel in the Settlement's after-school programs where the current behavior of the children became known. A majority of these children have siblings in treatment. Therefore, staff conferences usually include information about the child who terminated as a part of the discussion of family dynamics.

CONCLUSIONS

While premature termination of treatment left major areas of psychosexual conflict unresolved, these two children reached a level of self-development that enabled them to seek out and establish sustaining empathic relationships within an environment that is pathogenic and continuously disorganizing. As a result, they were able to maintain grade levels in school and significantly reduce their disruptive and delinquent behavior.

The importance of the child's current environment is highlighted by the results of this study. Though treatment was permitted by the parents and the children were able to respond and to develop in reaction to appropriate initial mirroring, protection, and gradual shifts in focus, deficiencies remained. It is interesting to note that the children signaled correctly the needed interventions. In their individualized treatment they led empathic therapists from primitive responses to more complicated interactions. In the end they terminated formal treatment and engaged themselves as best as possible with more benign adults and environments. They were signaling that an essential focus to assist their progressive development would have to be action upon and with their families and their external environments to curtail the pathogenic influence in their lives.

REFERENCES

Albert, A., Neubauer, P.B., and Weil, A.P. Unusual Variations in Drive Endowment. *Psychoanalytic Study of the Child*, 1956, 11:125–63.

Beres, D. Clinical Notes on Aggression in Children. *Psychoanalytic Study of the Child*, 1952, 7, 241–263.

Bettelheim, B., and Sylvester, E. Physical Symptoms in Emotionally Disturbed Children. *Psychoanalytic Study of the Child*, 1949, 3/4, 353–368.

Blos, P. Comments on the Psychological Consequences of Cryptorchism: A Clinical Study. *Psychoanalytic Study of the Child*, 1960, 15, 395–429.

De Hirsch, K. Language Deficits in Children with Developmental Lags. *Psychoanalytic Study of the Child*, 1975, 30, 95–126.

Eissler, K.R. Death Drive, Ambivalence and Narcissism. *Psychoanalytic Study of the Child*, 1971, 26, 25–78.

Freud, A. The Ego and the Mechanisms of Defense. *The Writings of Anna Freud*, Vol. II. New York: International Universities Press, revised edition, 1973.

Fries, M.E., and Woolf, P.J. Some Hypotheses on the Role of the Congenital Activity Type in Personality Development. *Psychoanalytic Study of the Child*, 1953, 8, 48–62.

Geleerd, E.R. A Contribution to the Problem of Psychosis in Childhood. *Psychoanalytic Study of the Child*, 1946, 2, 271–291.

Holder, A. Theoretical and Clinical Notes on the Interaction of Some Relevant Variables in the Production of Neurotic Disturbances. *Psychoanalytic Study of the Child*, 1968, 23, 63–85.

Kohut, H. Forms and Transformations of Narcissism. *Journal of the American Psychoanalytic Association*, 1966, 14, 243–272.

Kohut, H. The Psychoanalytic Treatment of Narcissistic Personality Disorders. *Psychoanalytic Study of the Child*, 1968, 23, 86–113.

Kohut, H. *The Analysis of the Self*. New York: International Universities Press, 1971.

Kohut, H. *The Restoration of the Self*. New York: International Universities Press, 1977.

Mahler, M. Notes on the Development of Basic Moods: The Depressive Affect. *Psychoanalysis—A General Psychology*, R.M. Lowenstein, L.M. Newman, M. Shur, and A.J. Solnit (Eds.). New York: International Universities Press, 1966.

Mahler, M. *On Human Symbiosis and the Vicissitudes of Individuation*. New York: International Universities Press, 1968.

Mittelmann, B. Motility in Infants, Children, And Adults: Patterning and Psychodynamics. *Psychoanalytic Study of the Child*, 1954, 9, 142–177.

Mittelmann, B. Motility in the Therapy of Children and Adults. *Psychoanalytic Study of the Child*, 1957, 12, 284–319.

Pavenstedt, E. The Effect of Extreme Passivity Imposed on a Boy in Early Childhood. *Psychoanalytic Study of the Child*, 1956, 11, 396–409.

Pine, F. On the Concept 'Borderline' in Children. *Psychoanalytic Study of the Child*, 1974, 29, 341–368.

Pumpian-Mindlin, E. Vicissitudes of Infantile Omnipotence. *Psychoanalytic Study of the Child*, 1969, 24, 213–226.

Rank, B., and MacNaughton, D. A Clinical Contribution to Early Ego Development. *Psychoanalytic Study of the Child*, 1950, 5, 53–65.

Ross, D., and Ross, S. *Hyperactivity: Research, Theory, and Action*. New York: John Wiley & Sons, 1976.

Spitz, R. Anxiety in Infancy: A Study of Its Manifestations in the First Year of Life. *International Journal of Psychoanalysis*, 1950, 31, 138–143.

Tolpin, M. On the Beginnings of a Cohesive Self: An Application of the Concept of Transmuting Internalizations to the Study of the Transitional Object and Signal Anxiety. *Psychoanalytic Study of the Child*, 1971, 26, 316–352.

Winnicott, D.W. Transitional Objects and Transitional Phenomena. *International Journal of Psychoanalysis*, 1953, 34, 89–97.

MARY E. WOODS

12

Childhood Phobia and Family Therapy: A Case Illustration

SINCE ITS BEGINNINGS in the 1940s and 1950s and until about a decade ago in some mental health and psychiatric circles family therapy was viewed as a renegade movement, led by turncoats (since many of its early leaders had been "traditionally" trained). To some psychoanalytically trained psychotherapists, "real" psychotherapy was one to one, often with the patient lying on the couch exploring intrapsychic issues. It followed, then, that family therapy was sometimes seen as less "deep" or, at best, primarily suitable for those with poor prognoses, or for patients unable to use psychoanalytic methods. On the other hand, some of those who jumped on the family treatment bandwagon began to look upon the individual as an illusion, with little or no identity apart from the ebb and flow of the family system; from this point of view, individual treatment often was seen as a futile exercise. Similarly, until recently, polarization dominated the relationship between child psychiatry and family therapy; the overlap was minimized and the differences were accentuated. (Malone, 1979)

To be sure, gradually family therapy has moved up the psychiatric totem pole and, today, the intertwining of internal psychological issues and external events is more widely recognized than formerly by most mental health workers. At the time of this writing, family treatment has become the fashion in many settings where it was repudiated or scorned only a few years ago.

But social work, from its earliest beginnings, and even during periods of intense preoccupation with either personality theory or social action, has consistently distinguished itself from other helping professions by its keen recognition of the interplay between people and their environments. Knowledge of the physical, economic, sociological, and family forces impinging on clients' lives— and how these interact among themselves and with the clients' particular personality characteristics—has been the raw material from which social work diagnoses and treatment plans have been formulated over the years. More than 60 years ago, Mary Richmond (1917) admonished that "no attempt to help a human being which involves influencing his mind in any degree whatsoever is likely to succeed without a knowledge of the Family Group of which he is a part, or without definite cooperation with that group." (p. 137) From then until now, certain shifts in emphasis notwithstanding, the person-in-situation concept, the concern with social functioning— i.e., the awareness of the interaction between the social and psychological aspect of human life, and the complex ways in which people and their environments influence one another—have been part of the social worker's basic knowledge (Bartlett, 1970).

Historically, it often happened that social workers were assigned to talk with the relatives of hospitalized patients or disturbed children, while psychiatrists saw the identified patients in individual therapy. It should be no surprise, then, that in 1970 40 percent of the practitioners treating families in groups were social workers, and that they constituted the largest single professional group engaged in family therapy (Group for the Advancement of Psychiatry, 1970). Ideas derived from systems theory, which have led to increased sophistication about the complex transactions that occur within families, generally were less foreign to social workers than to others. The basics of the biopsychosocial approach to diagnosis and treatment were well developed by social work before the family therapy movement took hold (Hollis and Woods, 1981).

There has been a tendency for some mental health professionals, including some social workers, to assume that to acccept one perspective is to deny the other. Therapy that relies on theories about personality development and intrapsychic processes has been considered by some to be irreconcilable with treatment that focuses on the observable transactions within a family unit. There are still some who see family problems only as the sum total of the difficulties of the family members. Those holding this view generally believe that individual therapy for each troubled person is the preferred approach. The opposite position asserts that understanding the individual—the person's dynamics and inner feelings—is neither necessary nor useful; if the person is to change, the therapist must promote shifts in the family system. Those holding this point of view also often look upon history-taking as irrelevant.

The family case example to be discussed here is one in which the worker made a multidimensional assessment. Inferences about the personalities and even unconscious conflicts of individual members were as important to the treatment as the appraisal of the family relationships, interaction, communication patterns, and myths. In no sense did the individual and family perspectives clash; indeed they complemented and required one another. There was no reason to choose between them.

A description of the the McCall family and the treatment will be followed by a discussion of the rationale that guided the worker's approach.

THE FAMILY TREATMENT

Deborah McCall had just turned 9 when she developed an acute, phobic preoccupation with snakes. She frequently dreamed and thought about them. She was afraid she would see them everywhere: in her closets and bureau drawers, under her bed, and on her way to school. Her parents, particularly her father, had attempted to reason with her; he patiently explained how unlikely it was that snakes would appear in the city apartment complex in which the family lived. He took his daughter to the zoo, where she could enjoy the large animals and birds, but she hysterically refused his urgings to enter the snake pavillion. He made several efforts to have her sit with him and look at pictures of snakes in the encyclopedia, but Deborah ran from him screaming, too frightened to look.

In addition, Deborah's previously lively interest in school had waned; she seemed subdued and tired much of the time. Although not very sophisticated about psychological matters, Deborah's parents were very alarmed by the sudden onset of their child's fearfulness and lethargy. When they realized that their efforts to help her to overcome them were not effective, they took her to a child psychiatrist.

The parents revealed a fairly unremarkable family history; Deborah's early development seemed to provide no real clues to her current problems. The child herself, extraordinarily articulate for her age, was unable to account for her fear, but was eager to be free of it. She said that she understood that her father was trying to help her to overcome it, even though his remedies were so frightening to her. She expressed good feelings about her relationships with her parents, yet was comfortable voicing complaints (e.g., she wanted a puppy but her parents refused because of limited space in their apartment). On the other hand, in her play with dolls in sessions with the psychiatrist, anxiety and hostility toward her parents were tapped.

Several months of treatment resulted in no symptom relief. Acting on the notion that the meaning of Deborah's difficulties might be uncovered in the family context, the psychiatrist referred the McCall family for family therapy.

Deborah's parents were black, Protestant, and middle class. Both parents had been raised in the large metropolitan city in the Northeast where they now lived in a quiet, integrated residential community. John was raised by grandparents after his mother died when he was 6. When his father remarried three years later, he insisted that John's mother should never be mentioned. Betty was the oldest of three children. When she was very young, her mother went to work, and Betty often had to look after her two young brothers. Although Betty did not complain as she talked about this, it was the worker's impression that circumstances had made it impossible for Betty to get much opportunity for play, or to be treated like a child.

The family did many things together and there were friends of long standing and contacts with extended family. John McCall was a college graduate who had advanced to a high supervisory position in a governmental agency. Mother, who had taught kindergarten before their only child was born, never returned to full-time work, but did some substitute teaching and was active in community organizations.

Deborah's relationships in school and with friends were excellent. From the first grade on she had attended an experimental school for intellectually gifted children. But recently she seemed to have lost interest in friends and was less outgoing.

John and Betty McCall, with their daughter, attended 30 family sessions over a period of eight months. During this phase of the treatment, there were also two joint sessions with the parents alone, and three meetings attended by Betty's parents, the Todds.

At the first family session the worker observed that the parents seemed to be very caring and respectful of one another, and both seemed very loving toward Deborah. No "underground" antagonisms were apparent. Expressions of appreciation of one another seemed genuine rather than defensive; shortcomings were discussed with perspective. In contrast to John, who was outgoing and frequently laughed and joked, Betty was more reserved, and often smiled quietly as others talked. Deborah seemed somewhat listless and preoccupied at times, but she could also be expressive and reflective. She knew her fear of snakes made "no sense," and she wanted to get over it. It was difficult to understand what had gone awry for a child in this family that seemed to be so well-balanced and able to express feelings of pleasure, love, and concern, and where good relationships among them were so obviously genuine.

Nevertheless, as the therapy proceeded, the worker sensed that the family climate was strained; an inexplicable feeling of apprehension permeated every session. The worker hypothesized that the uneasiness might derive, at least in part, from the family's reaction to her or to the therapy. Just as every action by a family member in some way reverberates upon the system, so the behavior and attitudes of the therapist become dynamic factors in the system of which he or she becomes a part. Specifically, because she was feeling bewildered by the family, the worker was becoming worried about whether she would be able to help the McCalls. She thought her anxiety about this might have spilled over into their meetings together. Or was there discomfort because the worker was white? As she encouraged feedback about her and the therapy, both John and Betty indicated that they felt comfortable with her. The said they felt that she was working hard—as they themselves were—to "decode" Deborah's symptom. In response to a direct question from the worker, the parents were emphatic that the color difference did not disturb them. Their positive attitudes and their interest in solving their problem were affirmed by their expressions of warmth to the worker and their regularity in keeping appointments.

The search for understanding continued. The worker noted that there was a family tendency to intellectualize at times, but it was not yet clear whether this was primarily a defensive, cultural, or idiosyncratic style. More apparent, the worker began to realize, was a repetitive communication pattern: Although the parents cooperatively answered questions about themselves, they usually returned quickly to discussing something about Deborah. There were times when John seemed to be almost compulsive in talking about or to the child.

The family seating arrangements seemed to hold some clue to the family structure and organization, but the meaning was not yet clear. For the first four sessions, John chose to sit on the couch next to his daughter, often putting his arm around her in what seemed to be a protective gesture. On the other hand, there were only occasional physical contacts between Betty and Deborah, and these were initiated by the mother when she wanted to tidy the child's hair or clothing. The worker noted that the parents were hovering over Deborah; this was hard to understand since in general Deborah did not seem to have been overprotected. Equally baffling was the fact that in spite of evidently authentic feelings of affection between the parents, there was no physical contact between them during sessions.

Once in response to a routine question about health, Betty reluctantly revealed that she had a heart condition–a fact that the parents had not shared with Deborah. The mother offered this information in a matter-of-fact, almost bland, manner, volunteering nothing further. With special caution, because she sensed she had uncovered a delicate matter, the worker sought to learn more about this. She found out that Betty had not even discussed her health problem with her parents; it was a carefully guarded secret indeed. Together, John and Betty had decided to keep the information from Deborah to avoid worrying her. For the first time an important source of tension contributing to the child's problems seemed to be emerging. The worker suspected that the mother's illness was more serious than either parent was acknowledging. She hypothesized that the child had intuitively realized that something frightening was happening, as the worker had, without knowing what was wrong. Since the meaning had eluded Deborah, she became symptomatic. She probably externalized her anxiety about the strained family atmosphere, and displaced her feelings of terror onto snakes.

Only after several sessions of sensitive exploration was it learned that the mother's increasingly weak heart could prove fatal, and that the parents feared (and had been told by their doctor) that it probably would. The prognosis was extremely poor and death could come at any time. As they talked together, the worker and family realized that Deborah's phobia had begun just a few weeks after Betty had been told about the seriousness of her illness, and after her parents had replaced their double bed with twin beds, ostensible because John was a restless sleeper and did not want to disturb Betty.

Once the family secret was fully revealed, the mood of the family meetings changed dramatically; family communications were freed and the inner feelings of all three came to the surface. Occasionally balanced by the impulse to deny or to hold on to some hope, John and Betty shared feelings of desperation and outrage. They all spoke of deep sadness and love. In a particularly moving session, Betty told her parents about her heart disease. She began taking more initiative than she had in the family meetings. She talked to her husband and daughter about some of her wishes for them "after I'm gone." About two months after Deborah was told about her mother's condition, her fear of snakes all but disappeared; it was revived only occasionally during bad dreams.

As a natural outcome of the greater freedom and sharing within the family, the rigid seating arrangements shifted. Sometimes mother and daughter sat together; sometimes John and Betty shared the couch and held hands throughout the session. The marital distancing that had followed the onset of Betty's illness had been replaced with renewed closeness. Greater softness and diminished reserve ("more the way it used to be," declared Deborah) were substituted for the subtle but pervasive uneasiness of early sessions. John was no longer so intently or exclusively fixated on Deborah or on protecting her.

The termination phase was particularly intense because the separation from the worker was experienced as a prelude to the family's loss of Betty, who seemed to be failing rapidly. Mourning had begun. Betty died less than a year after treatment ended.

TREATMENT RATIONALE

This case illustrates the intertwining of external and internal processes. The multidimensional assessment included: (1) existential observations of family interactions; (2) inferences about the inner lives, including unconscious phenomena, of family members; (3) an analysis of the interdependence of the past and the present; and (4) an understanding of the reciprocal influences of these, each upon the others. Of interest also was the awareness that particular events—including the onset of Deborah's phobia—served different functions at different levels. The discussion that follows elaborates on these points.

First, the family forces operating in the McCall case are an example of the purpose of family myths and secrets. They served the function for the family that defenses serve for individuals (Ferreira, 1963; Pincus and Dare, 1978). Facts and feelings were concealed, and fictitious notions about the family's well-being were advanced to keep conflicts, dreaded thoughts, or emotions outside of awareness, and to maintain the family equilibrium in the face of threats against it. The parents, truly believing they were protecting Deborah, consciously presented a false picture. They kept Betty's poor health a secret, and justified doing so by the myth that children are too vulnerable to assimilate the harsh facts of illness and death and must, therefore, be insulated from them. John and Betty were less aware that the urge to shield Deborah, and the "all-is-well" myth also were futile attempts to protect themselves from confronting the inevitable tragedy.

Second, Deborah's symptom itself acted as a family defense. Her fear of snakes provided a focus for the family whereby attention was diverted and fear about Betty's illness was externalized. It can be inferred that the phobia—as dramatic and upsetting as it was to them all—was less terrible than the issues it helped obscure. Although speaking specifically about school phobias, Lieberman (1979) could be describing other childhood phobias as well: "Generally, the phobia is complemented by the parents' problems and unconscious encouragement of the phobia" (p. 174). In this case parental support of the phobia (which conflicted with the conscious wish for Deborah to recover from her fears) was part of the defense. As long as they could worry about Deborah, they could keep their deeper concerns about Betty's impending death at a distance from their awareness.

Third, Deborah's phobia was more than a response to the terrible secret, or a defensive distraction for all family members. Psychodynamically, it seemed to reflect Deborah's inner reaction to the shift in the family interactions that followed the discovery of Betty's illness. According to Colm (1966), a child can become phobic when threatened with desertion, lack of approval, or inner feelings of hostility, or when feeling forsaken by parental insincerity. "It is against a *specific* background of *conflicting* anxieties on the part of his parents that a child develops a phobia"(p. 61). As Betty became weaker, quieter, and more withdrawn, Deborah's phobia was her way of masking the panic and rage prompted by this radical change in her formerly outgoing, affectionate mother.

Fourth, it was the worker's assessment that the phobia served to communicate yet another matter about which Deborah felt frightened and wanted help. It was revealed in one of the sessions with the parents alone that their sexual relations had diminished sharply following the diagnosis of Betty's illness. Betty was not making any overtures toward John, and he was afraid of overtaxing her. Beyond that, Betty had withdrawn from John in much the same way she had from Deborah. Seating patterns during sessions, and changes in sleeping arrangements mentioned earlier, were indications that physical distance had developed between them. When Betty began to retreat into herself, John turned to Deborah. His energy and need for solace were transferred, in part, from the marriage to the father–daughter relationship. He became more physically affectionate toward Deborah, and spent a good deal of time with her. On some level he may have even welcomed her need for help with her fears. It is important to emphasize, however, that John was not aware of the sexualized effect his behavior might have on Deborah; it was certainly reassurance and closeness he was seeking from his daughter, *not* sexual satisfaction.

But for Deborah, residual oedipal longings (e.g., "I wish I could get rid of mother and have father to myself") must have been exacerbated as she registered the fact that she was getting more attention from her father than her mother was. Her conflict about these unmanageable feelings was far easier to handle when projected onto *avoidable* objects, such as snakes. "City girls can fear and avoid those wriggly phallic objects with great ease" (Leherman, 1979, p. 1976). It would seem, then, that Deborah's phobia was not only an "SOS" in general terms—a communication that something was very wrong somewhere—but it also contained a very specific, symbolic message. Knowing that it is not uncommon for the fear of snakes to cloak anxieties about winning (or losing) the oedipal race, the worker followed the clue by arranging joint sessions with the parents to explore the status of their intimate relationship.

Fifth, knowledge of the past and understanding of its influence on individual family members in the present were also important to the treatment. For example, the fact that Betty was the oldest of three children, and was expected to take a lot of responsibility for her young brothers, suggested that she had probably learned very early not to make too many demands on others. Even in the face of fears about her own death, childhood circumstances and training— along with other factors already mentioned—contributed to her reluctance to express her feelings and ask for comfort from those who loved her. Similarly, John's personality was certainly influenced by early events, especially the loss of his mother. When confronted with the reality of his wife's illness, his need to evade his feelings about it was undoubtedly influenced by the fact that long ago he had had to put painful memories aside, particularly after his father remarried and forbade him ever to mention his father again.

This discussion brings us closer to a synthesis of intrapsychic and family systems theories. The McCall family case demonstrates that each individual in a family can be viewed as having a discrete personality with boundaries, however permeable, that contain the unique characteristics of that person. Whether derived from nature or from nurture, many of these individual qualities endure over time. In every family each member has his or her own peculiar temperament, talents, values, motives, impulses, and defenses, many of which were formed at a very early age. These attributes often survive in the face of family shifts—or, for that matter, even when there are changes in the person's larger social networks. Like the family, the personality system has its own style of reacting to stress and struggling to maintain the homeostatic balance of its system. Specific symptoms and reactions are a function of the individual's personality dynamics as well as an expression of his or her enmeshment in larger systems. For example, John's strong involvement with Deborah was triggered by changes in the family situation, but his choice of reaction reflected his individual psychology; he could have immersed himself in his work, and look for consolation there, or he could have had an affair. Similarly, Deborah could have become a bed-wetter or a disruptive student. Betty could have turned to Deborah for solace instead of withdrawing.

Family therapy concepts provide us with the understanding that family members are components in an interacting group, in which the actions of one member inevitably influence the others. But the *particular modes of response* are determined in part by the idiosyncratic characteristics of that person. Of course, these individual responses, in turn, reverberate upon the family system. (For instance, imagine how different the entire family climate would have been had John decided to handle his distress by having an affair.)

Working from a psychoanalytic/ego psychology perspective, the worker attempted to help each individual tolerate a broad range of feelings, and to confront some internalized conflicts and distortions, and externalizations of old introjects—some of which were brought out into the open and at least partially resolved. For example, Betty's fear, stemming from childhood experience, that requests of others may provoke anger or disapproval, was uncovered and tested against current reality. Similarly, John's assumption, emanating from his past, that sharing pain about loss with others was unacceptable, was discussed and put to rest in family sessions. Deborah's worry that her parents, who had always admired her excellent achievement in school, now thought less of her because her performance had deteriorated was exposed and corrected. Had there been less attunement to the specific personality and intrapsychic issues of each family member, important areas of individual work might have been neglected.

Grasp of the family system—of the interdependence of its parts, and of how the actions of each member become both cause and effect of the actions of the others—was equally essential. One member's internal event, once externalized, becomes part of the interactional field and an aspect of the environment of the other members. For example, Deborah's oedipal anxiety, which could be considered a discrete, internal issue, contributed to her snake phobia—which, in turn, had complex repercussions on the family as a whole, and also served a defensive function for the parents.

Systems' concepts provided the rationale for many of the interventions, designed to promote shifts in the family structure. By helping the parents to resume their former close relationship, and by helping Deborah and her mother to feel more relaxed with one another again, the overinvolved and frightening intensity of the father–daughter interactions was reduced, replaced by a more comfortable kind of intimacy. Participation by maternal grandparents was elicited in order to provide support for all members during Betty's illness. For Betty, the realization that she was losing everything called for as much comfort as possible from those whom she loved the most. For John and Deborah, the sense of continuity became important; reassurance about the future turned out to be as critical as acceptance of the approaching tragedy.

It seems evident that continued efforts to explore Deborah's fantasies and inner conflicts in individual treatment would not have had the same impact on her difficulties as family treatment did. Moreover, John and Betty would not have been helped at all had Deborah been the only family member in therapy. The problems of children, who so thoroughly depend on their family environment and yet usually have little power to influence it directly, are inseparably interwoven with the lives of other family members. When children's symptoms are presented, there is often no way of knowing exactly where the stress or pathology lies. Sherman (1966) notes that because the child's boundaries are fluid and interlaced with the outside world, particularly the family, we cannot be sure what is inside the child and what is outside. For children, symptoms almost always seem to be a communication about the family situation—a message that reverberates upon the system as Deborah's did, and one that must be deciphered if therapy is to help. Children's symptoms are usually best understood and treated in the context of the family.

In these days of innumerable new fads, gimmicks, "cures", and multiplying modes of treatment emerging from the mental health and related professions, a word should be added on the subject of symptomatic treatment. What about behavior therapy, hypnosis, or other methods designed to remove a particular symptom? Would any of them have been useful, or a more efficient means for eliminating Deborah's snake phobia? An answer to this question should take into account the fact that Deborah's fears can be viewed not only as a sign of distress, but also as a sign of health—hers and her family's. Given her parents' devotion to her, this child's symptom was a sure way of alerting them to the fact that she was in pain, and that there was trouble in the family. Had some kind of symptom-removal procedure been successful, it seems probable that the family's anxiety and despair would have been buried more deeply than they were and, once Betty died, the lack of resolution would have had long standing effects on Deborah, on John, on Betty's parents, and on their relationships with others.

Had the secrecy been maintained, had denial prevailed, surely Deborah would have been left with guilt, depression, and unresolved grief after the loss of her mother. And, of course, if she learned that her parents had deliberately withheld the truth from her, surely she would have been bitter that they had promoted the myth that all was well in her family while her mother was dying. Under these circumstances, Deborah's loss of her mother could have resulted in separation anxiety powerful enough to work its way down through generations to come (Leader, 1978).

Postscript on the McCall Family

Five sessions were held with John and Deborah after Betty died. Betty's parents, the Todds, joined two of these. Before father and daughter went to live a distance away with the Todds, there was a short time for all, including the worker, to share sadness, and for the now reconstituted three-generation family to plan for the future. It was fortunate for Deborah that, before her mother died, she had several months, in an atmosphere of trust and openness, to understand what was hapening, to have her questions answered, to learn that others were affected as she herself was, and to begin to integrate the impending loss. These opportunities freed her to recover, and even to grow, from the experience.

John, too, was able to grieve, to feel that he and Betty had said their goodbyes from a point of closeness, and to move forward to the next phase of his life less burdened than he otherwise might have been. Among many other benefits of the treatment was John's awareness of his need for adult companionship. Having been helped to recognize how he had overtaxed Deborah by turning to her for comfort during Betty's illness, he was alert to any tendency he might now have to look to his daughter to fill the place left by his wife's death. The importance of this for Deborah is obvious: She could feel safe in her relationship with her father at a time when she needed him more than ever.

For several years, from time to time, John dropped a note to the worker to say that he was doing well in every respect, and that Deborah was growing up "fantastically." Certainly, at some future point Deborah might feel the need to return to therapy, particularly since she had had such a positive experience in family treatment. However, the relatively short therapy apparently had been sufficient to help the family endure the tragic crisis together, to make shifts in disabling interactional patterns, and to free the relationships that had been stifled by secrets, myths, and each family member's private terrors. And, as John put it in one of his notes to the worker: "By sharing death so closely with Betty, Deborah and I learned a lot about life."

CONCLUSIONS

Several conclusions can be drawn from this treatment of one child in one family. Treatment began because of concern with Deborah's symptoms. However, therapy for the child—and ultimately for the entire client family—progressed because the importance of several interacting variables was assessed. Specifically, interventions were guided by the understanding of the relationship of the child's symptoms to the following.

1. *Family stress.* The child's symptoms were reactions to family stress derived from the cover-up of her mother's fatal illness.

2. *Family defense system* The child's symptoms were an integral

part of the family defense system. The latter sustained the symptoms so that the fears of each family member could be externalized.

3. *Changes in mother.* The symptoms were a specific reaction to the mother's withdrawal.

4. *Changes in father.* The symptoms were a symbolic response to the father's suddenly increased attention and physical contact with the child.

5. *Internal conflict.* The symptoms represented the child's particular mode of responding to a personal, internal conflict.

6. *A means of communication.* Deborah's symptoms were a child's understandable way of communicating at a time of distress. How can a child talk about that which is not understood, not explicit, and only felt? The ability to feel the family crisis and to respond was a sign of health; the family's ability to "hear" the child is also witness to its basic health.

Generally, circular casuality and complex interrelationships are vitally involved in human distress and human recovery.

REFERENCES

Bartlett, H. M. *The Common Base of Social Work Practice.* Washington, D. C.: National Association of Social Workers, 1970.

Colm, H. *The Existentialist Approach to Psychotherapy with Adults and Children.* New York: Grune & Stratton, 1966.

Ferreira, A. J. Family Myths and Homeostasis. *Archives of General Psychiatry,* 1963, 9, 457–463.

Group for the Advancement of Psychiatry. *The Field of Family Therapy.* Report no. 78, New York: Group for the Advancement of Psychiatry, 1970.

Hollis, F. and Woods, M. E. *Casework: A Psychosocial Therapy.* New York: Random House, 1981.

Leader, A. L. Intergenerational Separation Anxiety in Family Therapy. *Social Casework,* 1978, 59, 138–144.

Lieberman, F. *Social Work with Children.* New York: Human Services Press, 1979.

Malone, C. A. Child Psychiatry and Family Therapy. *Journal of the American Academy of Child Psychiatry,* 1979, 18, 4–21.

Pincus, L. and Dare, C. *Secrets in the Family.* New York: Pantheon, 1978.

Richmond, M. *Social Diagnosis.* New York: Russell Sage Foundation, 1917.

Sherman, S. Family Treatment: An Approach to Children's Problems. *Social Casework,* 1966, 48, 368–372.

Subject Index

Acceptance 117
Accountability 46-47
Acting out 62, 66
Adaptation, Failure of 81
Addiction 60, 64, 74
Adolescents
  Assessment of family 138
  Attitudinal changes 126
  Dependence 127
  Disturbance 127-128
  Drives 126
  Identity 126, 128
  Mixed age group 128
  Multiproblem family 137
  Narcissism 141
  Participation in therapeutic
    groups 125-126, 128
  Peer group function 127
  Placement of 138, 143-144, 148
  Relationship to family 144
  Resistance 140-141
  Self-image and identifications
    138
  Therapeutic techniques 141-149
  Treatment 138-149
    Treatment modes 127-128, 136
Aggression 151-152, (see also
    Hyperaggression)
Aging 95
American Group Psychiatric
    Association 38
American Orthopsychiatric
    Association 3, 38
American Psychoanalytic
    Association 38

Analysis (see Psychoanalysis)
Anxiety 61-62, 95, 97, 102, 137, 155,
    159, 161, 176
Assessment, Multidimensional
    167, 171
Authoritarian settings 6
  Involuntary treatment 115
  Relationships w/ authority
    figures 25, 34
Autoplastic symptoms 74
Avoidance 62

Bonding
  Developmental bond 79
  Separation processes 79, 80, 88
Boston Psychoanalytic Society 22

Curriculum: psychoanalytic 69
Children 77
  Abuse 60, 64
  Marriage disequilibrator 94
  Meaning of symptoms 172-173,
    175-176
  Phobias and family therapy
    165-178
Classifications 8
Client 5, 6, 8, 10, 15, 16, 17
  Improvement 6
  Repulsive 15
  Self-determination 24
Clinical Social Social Work
    Journal 17
Community
  Clinics 7, 8, 13, 15
  Psychiatry 11

Compulsive behavior 30
Confidentiality 10, 115
Conflict
  Anxieties 172
  Inner 30, 82
  Intra- or interpersonal 25
  Marital (see Marital)
  Relationships 152
Conjoint therapy (see Marital,
  Family therapy)
Counterculture 4
Countertransference 5, 56, 79, 88
  Family or conjoint therapy 101
  Mixed age group 129
  Reparation 79, 83-84
  With involuntary clients 116-117
Criminal offenders 109-21
  Acceptance 117
  Countertransference 116-117
  Diagnosis of adult offenders 112
  Empathy 112-114
  Force and clients' rights 111
  Motivation 110
  Obstacles to treatment 114-116
  Probation officers 115
  Resistance 111, 113, 118
  Sociocultural factors 114
  Therapist's responsibility to the
    court 115
  Value orientation 114
  View of treatment 115
Culture 4, 8, 12, 15

Decompensation 145
Defense 25
  Againt anxiety 61-62
  Appropriate 129
  Avoidance 62
  Family therapy 169, 177
  Hyperaggressiveness 155
  Identification 61
  Marital cases 96, 102-103, 106
  Mechanisms 57-58
  Repression 61
  Sexual preoccupations 130
  Symptom formation 60-68, 172
  Transference resistance 58

Delinquency 74
Dependency 24-25, 27, 29, 33, 81,
  103, 126-127, 140
Depression 95, 156, 176
Deprivation 31, 139
  And hyperaggressive behavior 151
Developmental theory 44-45,
  139-140
Diagnosis 7, 22-23, 30, 60, 110
  Of adolescents 138
  Of adult offenders 112
  Biopsychosocial approach 166
  Diagnostic theory 45
  Differential 40-41
Discrimination 8
Disease 8, 9
DSM-III 45

Education
  Clinical social work Foreword 2
  Generic Foreword 1
  Medicine 12
  Psychology 12
  (See Postgraduate training
    program)
Ego 57, 75, 82
  Conflict 152
  Defense 61
  Deficits 81
  Ego-syntonic atmosphere 75
  Growth 25
  Organization 161
  Psychology 138
  Support 33, 141
Emotional 7, 15, 128
Empathy 94, 117, 161, 163
Environment 8-10, 16-17, 33, 138
  (See "holding environment")
  Pathogenic 163
  (See Placement)
  Social 127
Evaluation 46-47 (See Assessment)

Faith healer 8
Family
  Interactions 171-173

Multiproblem (See
        Multiproblem families)
Secret 171-172
Separation difficulties 73
Structure 170
Therapy 73 (See Family therapy)
Family therapy 165-178
    Benefits of treatment 176-177
    Countertransference 101
    Effects on family 161
    Environment 175
    Family systems theory 174-176
    Individual therapy 166
    Interviews 92
    Meaning of symptoms 176
    Treatment of adolescent 142-145
Family Therapy Movement 30
Fantasies 147, 153, 156
    Sexual 66
Feminists 24
Fixations 75, 153, 161
Fusion
    Symbiotic 76

Grandiosity 154-155, 158, 160-161
Group
    Couples 101-102
    Family 102
    Focus 128
    Heterogenous 87, 91
    Mixed age group 128-136
    Transitional family 135
    Treatment of adolescents 128-136
Group for the Advancement of
    Psychiatry 5-8

Health 7-8
Holding environment 70, 80-83, 88
Hospital 7
Hyperaggression
    Children 151-164
        And identification 153
    Empathy in treatment of
        hyperaggressive children 160
    Goals of therapy 161
    Importance of environment 163

Identification 148
    Empathic 84
    "Identification with the
        Aggressor" 61-62, 153
    In group psychotherapy 128
    Internalized 138
    Hyperaggressiveness 153, 160
    With parents 126
Illness 7-8, 15
    Mental 7, 15, 33
    Of spouse 95
Insight 15, 91, 103
Insurance 13-14
Interpersonal theory 45
Introjection 80
Interviews
    Conjoint 103
    Family 97
    History-taking 92, 167
    Role-playing 25
Involuntary treatment (See
        Criminal offenders)

Jewish Family Service 30

Latency 127
Libidinal object constancy 79

Magical 155-156-158
Marriage 93, (See Marital)
Marital 15, 29-30
    Communication, lack of 94,
        104-105
    Conflict 91
    Conjoint therapy 103, 106
    Disequilibrators 94-96
    Motivation 96
    Partner substitution 95
    "Pre-stable" marriage 93
    "Pseudo-stable" marriage
    Relationship 101
    "Stable" marriage 93-94
    Stress 94-96, 102, 105
    Study-assessment and
        engagement 97-98

Therapeutic strategies: focal
    areas 98-100
  Modalities 100-102
  Techniques 91, 102-106
  Transactional patterns 96
  "Unstable" marriage 94
  Viewed by psychoanalytic
    development theory 92
Massachusetts General Hospital 23
Medical 9, 12
  In diagnostic theory 45
  Medical model 4, 6-10, 13
Mental
  Health 8
  Illness 8, 33
Modeling 25, 103
Mother
  Changes in 176, 178
  Death of 176-177
  "Rejecting mother" 53, 56, 60, 82
  Role 105, 134-135, 172
  Teenage 51
  Therapy 73
Mother-Child relationship
  Bonding and separation 79-80
  Conflict-free autonomous
    ego-functions 82
  Ego deficits 81
  Fear of closeness 76
  "Gradual failure of adaptation"
    81
  Narcissism 77
  Premature separation 77
  Protective shield 81-82
  "Primary maternal
    preoccupation" 81
  Rejecting mother 53, 56, 60,
    64, 67
  Symbiotic fusion 76-77, 80
  Trust 77
Motivation 6, 51, 57, 92, 96-97, 112
  Adolescents from multiproblem
    families 149
  Dealing with lack of 113-114
  Involuntary clients 109-111, 119
  Marriage goals 97, 105

Readiness for psychotherapy 109
"Unmotivated patient syndrome"
    51, 110-111, 137
M.S.W. 12
  (See Postgraduate training
    program)
Multiproblem families 51, 60
  Treatment of adolescent
    from—See Adolescents

Narcissism
  Individuation 77
  Narcissistic aggression 75
  Narcissistic behavior disorders
    74-76
  Narcissistic disappointments 159
  Narcissistic fixation 75
  Narcissistic injury 118
  Narcissistic mortification 153
  Narcissistic transference 75
  Of therapist 116
  Preoedipal patterns 75
Narcissistic Personality Disorder
    74-75, 153
National Association of Social
    Workers 11
  NASW Register 38
National Federation of Societies for
    Clinical Social Work
    (Acknowledgments),
    (Foreword 2), 37, 39, 43
NIMH 52
National Registry of Health Care
    Providers in Clinical Social
    Work 37-38
Nurturance 24, 27, 33, 59, 65

Object relations 156, 161
  Theory 77, 79
Organizational theory 45-46

Parent-Child 15, 28-30, 77, 168
  Father-daughter relationship 173
Parishioners 8
Pastoral counselor 8
Patient 6, 8, 9, 14-15

Person 10
Person-in-situation 22, 33
Personality 6, 10, 22, 167
Phobia
　In childhood 167, 172
　Symbolism 173
Physicians 8
Placement, Adolescents in 138-148
Postgraduate training program
　Auspices 42-43
　Clinical curriculum 47-48
　Core curriculum 43-47
　Evaluation of outcome 48
　Goals 40-42
　Skills 40-42
Poverty 8, (See Deprivation)
Practice theory 46
President's Commission on Mental
　Health
Preverbal disorders 75
Privacy 10
Private practice 45-46, 48
Probation officers 115, 119
Professions
　Bias against social work 21
Professional 6, 49, 166
　Education 37
　Professional attitude 82
　Professionalization of social
　　work 32
　Values and ethics 47
　Work with criminal offenders 110
Psychiatric 13
　Model 7
Psychiatrist 6, 12-13, 15, 168
Psychiatry 8-9, 15, 21, 165
Psychoanalytic 12, 52-54, 56-57,
　61-62, 66, 68-70, 75, 164, 174
Psychological 9, 12, 16
　Disorders 5, 8
　Intervention 7
Psychologists 11, 13
Psychology 12
　Analytic ego psychology 91
Psychopathology 7, 9, 61-62
　Developmental theory 44

Psychosocial 8, 16
Psychotherapist 5, 7, 10,
　See Therapist
Psychotherapy 3-6, 10-16, 40, 62
　Adolescents in placement 148-149
　Casework 22
　Definition 3
　Elements and objectives 39
　Medical model 4, 7, 10, 13
　Psychotic people 25
　Roots in social work 21
　Social work psychotherapy 12, 16,
　　17, 21
　Supportive 25
　Time phases 32

Reality, And transference 25-26,
　28, 34
Regression
　During adolescence 127
Relationship 5, 6
　Conflictual 152
　Countertransference
　　(See Countertransference)
　Empathic (See Empathy)
　Father-daughter 173
　In mixed age group therapy
　　134-135
　Marriage (See Marital)
　Parental 103
　Sexual 173
　Social 15, 40
　Reparation 84-88
　Teacher-student 70
　Therapeutic 25, 44, 55-57, 62, 88
　With parents, peers 168
Relocation 95
Reparation 84-88
Repression 61
Resistance 61
　Coping with (See Empathy)
　Of adolescents 140-141, 146
　Of therapist 116
　Transference resistance 57
　Involuntary clients 111-113, 118-119
Schizophrenic 64-65, 157

Secrets 98, 101, 103, 176-177
Self-determination 33
Self-image 25, 33, 95, 96
  Of adolescent 138
  Use of self
  Self-worth 59
Separation (See Separation-
  Individuation)
Separation-Individuation 94
  Developmental bond 79-80
  Dependence 80
  From family 135
  In adolescence 126
  In hyperaggressive children
    159, 161
  Libidinal object constancy 79
  Maternal consistency 80
  Separation and bonding 80, 88
  Separation difficulties 73, 101
  Subphases 81
  Premature separation 77
Sexual 66, 94, 102
  And drug use 66
  Preoccupations 130
Social 9
  Policies 10
Social work 9-10, 12, 15
  Accountability and evaluation
    46-47
  Clinical curriculum 47
  Developmental theory 44
  Diagnostic theory 45
  Distinguishing characteristics
    166
  Education 37 (See Postgraduate
    training program)
  Family group treatment 30
  Interpersonal theory 45
  Organizational theory 45-46
  Practice theory 46
  Psychoanalytic principles 68-70
  Skills 41
  "Social service" 24
  Specialization 48
  Treatment of families 166
  Values and ethics 38, 47

Social workers
  Direct service practitioners 8-9,
    11, 13-14, 16-17
  Definition of clinical 39-40
  Goals 24, 40-42
  Private practice 11, 12
  Respect of person 24
  Self-evaluation 41-42
  Value orientation 24
Social work psychology
  (Foreword 3)
  Differential diagnosis and
    treatment 40-41
  Functional approach 22
Socioeconomic 4
Society 10, 14
Sociological 12, 16
Stigma 8, 119
Stress 8-9, 31, 33
  In adolescent 146, 177
  Marital 94-96, 102, 105
Supervision 11-12, 32, 34, 48-49, 83,
  85, 117
  And psychoanalytic theory 69
Symbolic recapitulation 77
Symptom 15, 177
  Communication 176, 178
  Diagnostic theory 45
  Phobia (See Phobia)
Synchronization 83
Systems, Family systems theory
  174-176

Therapist 6, 16-17, 32, 79, 82-83, 86,
  149, 167, 169
  Family 93
  Gratifications 117
  Limits and controls 141-142
  Marital 101, 106
  Narcissism of 116
  Object tie with 77
  Patient relationship 55-57
  Responsibilities to judicial 115
Therapy 6, 17
  Ambivalence 92-93, 97
  Biofeedback 4

Checkmated therapy 84
Emotional 4
Goals 5, 161
Group 87, 127
Individual therapy 97, 165-167
Insight 15
Marital (See Marital)
Psychopharmacological 4
Resistance 113-114
Self-help 4
"Therapeutic alliance" 55-56, 106,
    112, 117
Therapeutic holding
    environment 82
Therapeutic relationship 62,
    113, 119
With adolescents
    (See Adolescents)
With criminal offenders:
    Overcoming resistance
    113-114_
With families
    (See Family
    therapy)
Transference 25-26, 28, 52-59
And resistance 57-58, 75
In marital therapy 101-103
Narcissistic transference 74-75
Negative transference
    55, 74, 97, 111
   In unmotivated patients 111
Object transference 75
Treatment
Expectations 59
Involuntary 109, 111, 114
Offenders view of 115
Right to 4
Right to refuse 111
Symptomatic 176
Time limits 32, 162
Utilizing transference as
    metaphor 26

Unemployment 8

Value systems 33, 38, 47

Author Index

Ahmed, P. I. 8
Austin, L. 6, 15, 21

Bergin, A. E. 3, 4
Bibring, E. 4
Brown, B. S. 7
Bruch, H. 3

Carkhuff, R. R. 4
Coelho, G. V. 8
Coleman, J. R. 6, 9, 21

Deutsch, L. 7

Epstein, L. 5

Falck, H. S. 16
Feiner, A. H. 5
Feldstein, D. (Acknowledgments)
Ford, D. H. 3-5
Fox, R. E. 6
Frank, J. 5, 9, 13
Freud, S. 14, 44, 57, 75, 126
Fromm, E. 5
Fromm-Reichmann, F. 5

Garrett, A. 3, 5, 13
Goldberg, A. 7
Gordon, J. S. 9
Gottesfeld, M. (Acknowledgments), 5
Gunderson, J. G. 3

Hamilton, G. 6, 21, 30
Harper, R. A. 15
Hollis, F. 9, 16, 21, 30

Jarrett, M. 11

Kleinman, A. 15
Knoll, D. 13
Kolker, A. 8

Leifer, R. 7, 13
Lessler, K. 6
Lieberman, F. Foreword xi, 15
Littner, N. 16
London, P. 7, 11

Marmor, J. 4
Marshall, E. 4
Mosher, L. R. 3

Parsons, T. 15
Perlman, H. 13, 30
Pinkus, H. Foreword xi-xii, 39

Rapoport, L. 14
Reynolds, B. 11
Richmond, M. 10
Robitscher, J. 8

Schorr, A. L. 8
Selye, H. 8
Simon, B. K. 9
Slaby, F. 7
Strean, H. 4, 6, 16
Strole, L. 15
Strupp, H. H. 3-4, 6
Szasz, T. 7
Sullivan, H. 5

Tancredi, L. 7
Towle, C. 4, 25, 31, 33, 37-38
Truay, C. B. 4
Turner, F. J. 17

Urban, H. B. 3-5

Wolberg, L. 3

Yarmolinsky, A. 13